Edited by R.E. Loten

Castle Priory Press

CASTLE PRIORY PRESS

First published in Great Britain in 2022 by Castle Priory Press, Brightlingsea

ISBN 978-1-7398867-5-2

Cover design: Jane Langan

For the Lido family, without whom there would be no Lido to write about

INTRODUCTION

When I took up the Writer in Residence role in November 2021, no-one (including me) was quite sure exactly what the role would involve. The only things I knew for sure were:

- I planned to write a series of books set in a fictional version of Brightlingsea, which would feature the Lido
- I wanted to organise an anthology of creative writing based around the Lido, which could be sold to raise much-needed funds for the Lido.

As I write this introduction, the first book in the series is being edited (I'm hopeful that it will be published later this year), the second book is planned and the anthology is almost ready for printing – not bad for less than six months in the job!

Seriously though, none of this would have been possible without the contributions of some incredibly talented writers. One of the things I wanted to use my role to do, was to encourage people who didn't believe they could, to write. I'm a firm believer that everyone has the ability to write a short story – all they need is a little help and guidance. So, during Winterfest, that's exactly what we did. The 'Introduction to Short Story Writing' workshop was where some of the pieces in this anthology sprang into life and I couldn't be prouder of those authors.

I also had the privilege of going into Brightlingsea Primary School to work with some of their students and teachers on their stories. Some of the best ones are featured in this anthology. The loveliest part for me, was that every single child engaged with the story writing process and came up with some fantastic ideas in the process – the next generation of authors is right there!

Authors are not, on the whole, sociable creatures. We are usually found scribbling away in some dark corner, growling at anyone who drags us out of our fictional world. Thus, it was with a degree of trepidation that I agreed to spend one day a week working in the Lido café. However, it has been an incredible experience so far. I get to talk to people about my writing, sell my books and spend far too long stroking all the gorgeous dogs who come to visit. If I'm really lucky, I even get a cuddle with Max!

If you'd like to talk to me about the anthology or any other writing-related matters, I can be found in a corner of the Lido Café most Fridays or you can contact me directly via email: lidowriter@gmail.com

I've waffled on for far too long (force of habit for a writer, I'm afraid!) so I will leave you with one final thought. This anthology is to celebrate 90 years of our Lido. We are a community and this book reflects what a fabulously creative one we are. Each piece is so different to the others and yet they are all, in one way or another, linked to and inspired by the same building.

All that's left for me to say now is, 'Dive in and enjoy!'

Ruth Loten

HISTORY

Lido: public open-air swimming pool or pleasure beach (Concise Oxford Dictionary)

The golden age of British lidos was in the 1930s. As outdoor swimming grew in popularity, they sprang up all over the country, only to close again as it gradually fell out of fashion. In the early 21st century, there was a move to re-open many of them, as once again, people began to consider the physical and mental health benefits of swimming outside.

Brightlingsea Lido (originally Brightlingsea Open Air Swimming Bath) was built as part of a scheme designed to improve the recreational facilities in the town. It was funded by a grant from the government's Unemployment Grant Committee as part of a national effort to provide much needed work for unemployed men and the grand opening took place on 23rd June 1932.

However, by 2017 its future was very much in doubt as Tendring Council made the decision to close it. A group of volunteers came together with a very different plan in mind and the Lido was relaunched as a local enterprise in 2018. Funding was secured to improve the facilities and in spite of the best efforts of Covid-19, four years later, it's still going strong with plans for further improvements already set in motion.

Further details on the history and future plans for the Lido can be found in the information leaflet available in the Lido Café or on our website: www.brightlingsealido.org.

CONTENTS

Lionel
by Tracy Brown

Lionel sat quietly by the window. The sun shone through creating a warm break from the icy blast outside as he took in his surroundings. Every table was taken; it was obviously a popular meeting place for all ages. Mums gathered after the morning school run, some with their younger babies clambering to get out of the buggy, other little ones sleeping undisturbed by the hubbub, allowing their mother that welcome moment of relaxation. Dog walkers, stripped from their hats and warm coats appreciating the break from the blustery weather, while their companions looked on from under the table, waiting for a treat of a cold sausage, or a crafty nibble of a piece of cake snuck under the table by a nearby dog lover.

Comforting and sociable.

The arrival of brunch broke Lionel's thoughts. The mouth-watering smell of a bacon sandwich arriving at his table, presented by a friendly smile, gave him a warm contented feeling. No judgements, no criticism, just a smile.

Lionel never made 'waves'. He was unassuming and kind and liked by many. He loved routine but felt frustrated by how it made his life tedious. He wanted life to be thrilling. He wanted to be impulsive, but his lack of confidence made him overthink things to a degree where he never actually got around to doing anything spontaneous or exciting. Even his name was boring. Lionel. Why wasn't he given the name Storm, or Maximus? Real masculine names. But no, Lionel was his name, and it conjured up his nature. Boring!

Finishing his sandwich and blowing the steam from his newly ordered hot coffee, the clinking of the crockery and the piercing scream of the coffee grinder interrupted his daydreams and brought him back into his surroundings. An exchange had taken place while he had been absorbed in his thoughts, and there were now eight older folk, moving furniture around, scraping the table and chair legs across the floor, causing a laughable mayhem as they got themselves settled. Friends. Seemingly lifelong long friends.

As they chatted, Lionel couldn't help but eavesdrop. They were reminiscing about the surroundings. The café sat on the site of the once simply known 'swimming pool', now more prestigiously known as 'The Lido'. A substantial sized open-air, cold-water swimming pool visited by crowds in the summer months but currently closed up for the winter.

With the conversation taking different paths amongst the 8 of them, but all related to the Lido in 'their' day, Lionel found it difficult to keep up and hear everything, but he heard snippets. 'Wooden slide' and 'matting' on the dive boards. 'Wooden sides covered in seaweed'. He was intrigued. He kept listening. It seemed most of them had learnt to swim in this pool, with it historically being one pool with a gradual slope to get in, rather than the 'baby pool' and 'big pool' it was now. To be honest, Lionel thought it sounded a bit grim, with the talk of slime on the bottom and crabs walking over their feet, but they were all laughing and enjoying the memories. A couple of them even found their first loves there.

Did they just say they stored oysters over winter? Surely not?

They noticed him listening. He felt ashamed and wanted the floor to open up under him. He apologised for being rude. One of them, a portly gentleman with a ruddy complexion and wearing a burgundy tank-top, stood up. Lionel felt himself redden. *Now I'm for it.*

The man introduced himself as Bob. Gesturing with his hands, he invited Lionel to join them! Lionel felt so embarrassed. He hadn't meant to interfere. They looked so happy and full of life. They were mesmerizing. He swallowed, stood up, picked up his chair and gently placed it into the space made for him. Bob introduced everyone. Lionel tried to remember each of them. Becky with short greying curly hair and a pink scarf, used to work in advertising. Charlotte, dark eyes, stripy hat and bangles – sort of hippy like. Mike, glasses, liked sport, especially endurance sports (something that Lionel was fascinated by). Graham, like himself seemingly shy, still shook his hand and smiled. Fliss; gregarious, bossy, friendly. Pip nodded a welcome (Lionel presumed his name was Phillip but he was introduced as Pip); bearded, dark blue woollen jumper, looked like he'd be comfortable on a barge, and lastly Dot. She was a homely looking lady with a large Lurcher named Olive, who was squeezed in between her owner and Bob.

Lionel introduced himself and again apologised. They welcomed him and all started to question him. Lionel answered, yes, he lived on the outskirts of town and had done so for about 12 years. Yes, he worked from home for a commercial sales company based in the city. No, he had no close family anymore. He had looked after his mother until she died 13 years ago, then he upped sticks and moved here. He'd never had the chance previously to get out much, and living in a city, added to his isolation. Moving here was the best thing he had done. He had been welcomed and (he thinks) due to his quirky looks and dress sense, he was becoming a 'character of the town'. He didn't mind, he wanted to be noticed. He wanted others to realise he had a sunny personality. Even if he was quiet. *It might, if he's lucky, create him some friends.*

Gradually the questions turned into a natural conversation. The friends had all grown up here, and now they were all in their 60's and 70's, and mostly retired. They met on occasion, like today, for a catch up. The time flew by.

After while they all said their goodbyes and departed. Lionel put on his yellow scarf, and his yellow crash helmet, adjusted his red rimmed glasses and headed outside to his trusty steed. Malcolm the mountain bike.

Pedalling towards home, Lionel felt elated. He'd had a magnificent morning, learning about the history of the Lido and the interesting lives led by his newfound 'friends'. Despite not having any contact details for them, he hoped to see them again at some point.

He whistled all the way home.

Once home, the quiet struck him. This was it. Apart from his work, this was his life. Quiet, dull, lonely.

His new friends seemed to lead such adventurous exciting lives, it made his appear all the more restrained. He needed to do something, but what?

He was fit, he was financially secure, and he was willing. But he was scared.

Lionel looked at himself in the mirror. *What are you scared of? Failing? You're failing anyway. You wanted to be a superhero remember?* He gave his reflection a stern look, straightened his glasses and stood tall.

'Time to take action' he said aloud. 'Let's do this'.

He spent the rest of the day scouring magazines and wracking his brain for exciting things to do. Sports? Events? Challenge? He wanted it to include the very place that led to the change in his thinking. The Lido.

Eventually he decided to try to do it all. He'd organise a triathlon!

He needed a Grand plan.

That night Lionel found it hard to sleep, the excitement and ideas spinning through his head. Numerous times he sat up in bed and jotted a few things down in his notebook to clear his head and act as a reminder in the morning.

'Distances of triathlon'
'Speak to Council'

'Advertising'

In the morning, he was still as enthusiastic. Where to start? He thought of Becky and Mike from yesterday. They'd be able to help him or answer some of the many questions, but he had no way of contacting them, and no idea when or if he would see them again. His confidence began to wane.

He put on his yellow bike helmet and his scarf and cycled down the road, not really knowing where he was heading but hoping to see someone from yesterday, or something to re-spark his vision. He steered towards the council offices. They were closed for another hour. He began to feel more defeated and self-critical. *What are you doing? How on earth are you going to organise a triathlon? You're a fool!* He pushed his bike towards a nearby bench and sat pondering. *Am I being silly? Are people just going to laugh at me?* He decided to keep trying for today and see how he felt that evening. *One day*, he told himself, *just one day. Even you can be brave for that long. Nothing ventured, nothing gained. It's not like you have anything else on today, after all.*

While he was waiting for the council offices to open, he called at the stationers. He bought a yellow notepad and a mustard-coloured biro (they didn't have bright yellow). Well, he thought to himself, if I'm going to do this, I need the right equipment. He looked up 'triathlon distances' on his phone and recorded it in his new notepad. Considering the size of the Lido and its surroundings, and the general public he wanted to aim his challenge towards, he deemed a 'sprint triathlon' to be the most fitting.

750m swim, 3.1mile run and 12.5mile bike distance.

The council office opened and he left a message regarding his event asking if he would need permission. Someone would get back to him.

He began to feel slightly more motivated.

He climbed onto Malcolm and sped his way towards the Lido, hoping for more inspiration. He'd need measurements of the pool and a track for the run and bike race. He needed marshals and probably First Aid stations, and refreshments, and start and finish posts, and advertising, and, and, and… Oh what was he doing?

Lionel decided to have a quick coffee in the Lido café and make a task list. Hopefully getting a little more organised, would make his mission less daunting.

Coming out of the café and about to climb back on his bike, he saw a big dog bounding about on the green like a spring lamb. 'Olive, Olive, come here,' shouted a familiar voice. It was Dot! Sprinting towards her, Lionel lost all his inhibitions and shouted her name as loud as he could. She looked up, squinting in his direction, before a huge smile of recognition crossed her face.

'Hello Lionel,' she said, 'are you ok?'

Lionel started gabbling, his words falling over themselves in his eagerness to explain his plans and newfound confidence.
'Ooh, slow down', she said, 'let's go for a cuppa and you can start from the beginning'.

Lionel explained how their spirit and gusto for life had rubbed off on him yesterday and how it had led to his plans for a triathlon. Dot's face came alive with sheer joy and encouragement.

He was reassured by Dot saying she would put him in touch with Becky and Mike. He felt even more encouraged when she told him that the whole group would likely be willing to support him.

Lionel felt he flew home on a bicycle with wings. He was ecstatic.

Over the following week, Becky offered to take care of all the advertising through social media and try to arrange estate agent sponsorship boards. Mike said he would speak to the clubs he belonged to, to drum up supporters and look into the safety issues. Graham, it turned out, had been an accountant, and agreed to look after the finance side of things. All of this help, but each of them allowed Lionel to maintain his lead in the project and be co-ordinator. He'd never had the courage or confidence to do anything like this before, and he couldn't quite believe how it was all progressing at such a rate. He'd even been given all their mobile numbers.

He decided to set a date of the last Saturday in September for the event. The pool would normally have not long closed for the season, but the committee had agreed (as any profits were going to the lido) to extend the opening and keep that day just for his triathlon. He was informed by the council that they were unable to close the road but, his event didn't need permission to go ahead, as long as he followed health and safety advice.

He had been told of the length and width of the pool (50m x 20m) so he could calculate the distance needed for the swim – 15 lengths. He already knew the distance from the lido to All Saints church and back along the seawall was six miles, so, he decided to reduce the mileage of the suggested sprint triathlon bike distance, by half a mile and use that route twice over – 12 miles. It was after all, a more cross country, rougher triathlon than the usual smoother professional ones. The outside perimeter of the Lido would be used for the run. Up one path by the green, along the seafront, back down the path by the boating lake and along the pavement back to the café. They'd need to run this lap 18 times to make the three-mile distance required.

Sorted!

As the time moved on through Spring and into Summer, people became more aware of the event. Lionel heard different mutterings.

'Ooh that sounds good'.
'You wouldn't catch me doing that'.
'Shall we give it a go?'

Of course, Lionel found himself focusing on the 'you wouldn't get me doing that' and again began to worry. It was such a big thing for him and so out of character. Should he stop now? But then he'd be letting those people down who had put themselves out for him. *Why did I start this? What if no one shows up? I'll never be able to show my face again.* He frowned. He had to think positively. *The others agree it's a good idea. The advertisements are everywhere and people are talking about it. People will come.*

On the day of the event, Lionel was up at the crack of dawn. He felt ill. Sick to the stomach. So worried. So scared. He couldn't eat breakfast. He paced up the hallway, past the Airfix planes hanging from the ceiling, turned at the Smiley doormat and paced back again. He stepped out the same route over and over again, muttering to himself, trying to think of excuses not to go. His phone pinged. It was Dot.

'We're outside'

He had arranged to meet 'the gang' by the lido at 07.30 to set things up, but they obviously knew how anxious he'd be feeling, and they'd come to get him. Should he hide? Should he answer the door? *Oh Lionel, grow a pair!*

'LIONEL' Dot was calling through the letterbox. She'd seen him. He'd have to go now. He gingerly opened the door and there they all were, bundled into a pale green Morris minor, obviously belonging to Charlotte, with a sunflower hanging off the aerial. In front of it a silver Peugeot 405 estate, with Olive packed into the very back with all the bunting and paraphernalia needed for the day.

Travelling towards the venue with a foreboding fear of failure, Lionel was close to tears. The chatter and the smell of fresh cakes and pastries, packed into plastic boxes to make up a picnic, were lost on him. He stared at the floor, littered with crumbs and dried mud. Petrified.

Approaching the Lido, Bob pressed the hooter, then again, and waved excitedly, as did Dot. Lionel dared himself to look up. There seemed to be quite a few people about. Dog walkers? Then it dawned on him. They were volunteers coming to help! Hordes of them!

His tears ran free. Tears of relief. Even if nobody turned up to do his triathlon, enough people believed in him to turn out and help set up.

Before long, row upon row of colourful bunting adorned the lido, directional posters and start and finish posts were placed, crates of bottled water, registration forms and medals boxed on the foremost table. The first aiders, first responders and route marshals sipping coffee, chatting and laughing made for a wonderful atmosphere.

A man in his thirties hovered, seemingly searching for someone. Lionel approached and was shocked when the man asked where he should sign in. 'Oh! Ah, erm, erm, follow me'.

Lionel's hand shook as he wrote 'Patrick King', along with his contact and next of kin details. A volunteer named George was at hand to show Patrick where to put his bike, his running shoes and the rest of his equipment, and where to store his day clothes until the race was finished.

After signing up Patrick, Lionel didn't leave his seat again until registration closed 15 minutes before the race was due to start. One hundred and twelve people signed up, many of them bringing family and friends for support and cheerleading. Queues for tea and coffees, cakes and bacon butties; Lido staff and volunteers all so busy, but smiling and laughing, taking it all in their stride, while competitors started jumping and stretching to warm up as they entered the pool area.

One hundred and twelve pairs of running shoes lined up in numerical order matching their owner's registration number. One hundred and twelve bikes held in a pen on the green, again in the same numerical order.
One very proud co-ordinator, dressed in a bright yellow T shirt, bought for him by eight friends, with the words 'Some people don't believe in superheroes, but they've never met LIONEL'

Lionel. Triathlon organiser. Friend. Superhero.

Can We Go To The Lido, Mum?
by Lucy Weaver

The sun is out but it's a sweltering day,
And we're running out of cooling games to play,
The paddling pool would take hours to fill,
And I'm beginning to slowly lose the will!

Then my little one pipes up with an idea,
One that makes me internally cheer,
'Can we go to the Lido, Mum?
I'm sure that lots of my friends would come!'

'Yes!' I reply as I picture the scene,
The Lido with its cooling waters so clean,
We quickly pack up our costumes and floats,
(We definitely won't need our coats!!)

Then we rush down to the beach and join the queue,
Waiting to dive into that water so blue,
From inside we can hear screams of delight,
And as we enter, we're greeted with a glorious sight...

People splashing and yelling and happily playing,
Folks dotted around on sun loungers laying,
Chatting with friends, meeting others they know,
At the place where the people of Brightlingsea go

We quickly get changed then jump straight in,
My daughter's face wears a permanent grin
She glides through the water and giggles with glee
It's a joyous scene I'm so happy to see.

We swim and we play then enjoy an ice cream,
And for just a few hours I'm living the dream,
It feels like a holiday but without going abroad,
And a break from the constant cries of 'I'm bored'

Sadly, our visit is over too soon,
As the light starts to fade and evening looms,
So we pack up and leave, but feel happy and chilled,
And my cup of life has been refilled!

Frank
by Dave Griffiths

Frank shuffled down the aisle, anxious to get to a seat before the bus jolted into motion. He had asked the driver of the bus, the number 62 from Colchester to Brightlingsea, to tell him when the bus was closest to the Brightlingsea Lido. The driver had snapped back a quick 'why don't you just google the place,' but then he had bitten back the remark. Presumably he'd seen the confused look on Frank's face.

Frank had called Sharon, and she had told him '… look Dad, why don't you just piss off. You haven't wanted any contact in all these years. Why bother now?' Then she had grudgingly sent him a small photo of her son, Ben, and told him that the boy was now 16 years old and typically hung out at either the Lido or on the seafront at a place called Bateman's Café.

Frank had drawn some money from his savings account. He told the staff at his assisted living accommodation that he was going away for a few days. They asked him where to, but he didn't say. He'd put a few things in a holdall, called a taxi, took a train. He bought a one-way ticket. It seemed sufficient.

The bus driver shouted to Frank that he needed to get off at the next stop, just outside the Co-op. He said that the Lido was straight ahead... a few hundred yards. 'Just follow your nose, mate,' he said. 'You'll smell the sea.'

Frank thanked him, climbed carefully down the bus stairs, set off walking. It was a warm, sunny afternoon. He saw a pub called the Railway just over the road. It looked like it had retained its old charm back from when the railway line (presumably) still ran into Brightlingsea. It didn't do that anymore. If it had, Frank would have got a ticket to here directly.

Frank had never been here before. He'd never even been to this part of the country before. He'd stayed in a room above a pub in Colchester the night before. The town had worried and frightened him. It was too noisy, too busy. He was too old for it. He wondered if he'd made a big mistake. Brightlingsea, however, seemed a lot calmer. A lot quieter. It felt peaceful.

He saw a sign for the Lido. Three hundred yards up the road. He thought he could manage that.

Ben and his friend Josh were sitting in the Lido café. They both had a can of Coke. Josh had picked a table with a view through to the pool. He was watching Cloe. She was splashing around in the shallow children's pool area with two of her friends. Josh would always try to meet up with Cloe after school. He would hang about in the hope that when she came out, he would be right there, and then he would start walking nonchalantly beside her. He didn't want to be pushy. He hoped she might look up and see him. He hoped she might smile and wave.

Ben noticed an old guy come walking into the café. He looked frail. He was struggling to open the door. The door had a strong spring. It needed quite a push to get it open, and the old guy looked like he might not manage it. Ben smirked, then turned back to Josh. 'Why don't you go get some trunks on and join them?' Ben asked. Josh looked shocked. 'I … I couldn't,' he spluttered. 'What if … well … she might …'

Ben laughed at his friend's discomfort.

The old guy was looking at them. He'd ordered a coffee, then he'd taken an envelope out of his coat pocket. He was studying the contents. Then he was peering over towards the two boys. His eyesight must be poor. He was staring … squinting at them.

'Piss off, old man,' Ben said. 'You some sort of perv or something?'

The old man looked away. He looked both embarrassed and disappointed.

'What's with you?' Josh said. 'No need to be rude. He's done you no harm.'

'You taking sides with the old pervy bleeder?'

Josh watched the old man get up. A girl was just bringing his coffee over, but he walked past her and back out of the café, struggling to get the door open again. He muttered 'sorry' to the girl as he went. She said something about putting it in a take-away cup, but the old man had gone. Josh didn't think the old man could have carried a take-away cup safely anyway. He looked so unsteady on his feet.

'So, you taking sides, then?' Ben repeated, obviously unwilling to let this go.

Josh didn't like Ben when he got like this. He would flare up, get in a mood. And then he couldn't back down. Josh looked back out through the window into the pool area. Cloe and her friends had gone. Josh turned back to his friend.

'Look, Ben. You're in a bad mood, and I really haven't got time for it. I'm going. Maybe catch you later ... but for God's sake try to relax. Take your foot off the bloody throttle for a while.'

Josh shook his coke can. It was empty. He left it on the table, then stood up and went out of the café. He said 'bye Olivia' to the young girl behind the counter. She smiled back at him and gave him a little wave. Funny, he thought. He could quite easily talk to Olivia. She was the same age as him. She was in his English class. She lived just down the road from him. They could easily walk to and from the school together, but he never waited for her outside school. Yet ... when he did see her, he could talk to her easily. He didn't stammer. He wasn't lost for words. She always smiled when she saw him.

Why couldn't he be like that with Cloe, he wondered.

. . . .

Ben left the Lido café. He was pissed off with his mate Josh. 'Maybe catch you later,' Josh had said. Yeah, well. Maybe not. Fuck him.

He set off walking the short distance down towards Bateman's Café. Not so much a café anymore. More a burger van but facing the sea. It offered hot drinks, cokes, ice-creams and burgers. Ben would sometimes come down here, get himself a drink and sit on the sea wall. He liked to watch the sea. He liked it whatever the weather ... quiet and calm, like it was today, or grey and blustery, the wind scudding the tops off the waves. He found the place calming.

Ben bought himself a can of coke ('can you drink too much coke' he asked himself) and went to sit on the sea wall. There was a little shelter you could sit in. A bit like one of those village bus-stops. He would sit in there if it was raining, but not today. Calm and sunny. He would sit on the wall.

He noticed the old guy was sitting in the shelter. He was looking out to sea. Ben pinged the top off his coke can. The old guy must have heard. He turned to look in Ben's direction.

'Fuck off, you pervy bastard,' Ben shouted across to the old guy.

The old man struggled to stand up, levering himself slowly off the wooden bench. He started to make his way towards Ben, walking across concrete path and then onto the section of sand. He was finding it hard to pull his way through the sand. It was as if he couldn't lift his feet high enough, couldn't pull them out of the small depressions his shoes made.

'Didn't you hear me?' Ben said, standing up, squaring up to face the old guy.

The old man continued walking towards Ben. Slowly. So slowly, But with grim determination.

Ben looked around. There was no one else on the beach. If he hit the old guy, there would be no-one around to witness it. He smiled to himself.

'Your name's Ben, isn't it?' the old man said.

'What the fuck's it got to do with you?'

'Your mum told me you might be here.'

The old man shuffled along and leaned against the sea wall. He didn't look as though he could stand much longer.

'Your mum, Sharon … she's my daughter. I haven't seen her in a while.'

Ben took a few steps away from the old man.

'We lost touch. I should have … well, you know. I should have been … '

The old man took the envelope out of his pocket. He pulled the small photograph out, holding it out for Ben to take it. Ben stepped forward and took the photo. It was picture of himself. Took maybe a couple of years earlier. He turned the photo over. On the back, in his mum's handwriting, it said 'Ben... 14 years old.' On the bottom of the photo, she had written the date the photo was taken, and she had signed it and drawn three little hearts.

'I called her last week,' the old man said. 'She told me to piss off.'

Ben smiled. He could well imagine his mum saying that.

She didn't want to tell me anything about you, but then I explained about … about … and so she …'

'About what?' Ben said.

'It's not important, but I just thought it would be nice to meet you. While there's still time.'

Ben grunted.

'You are probably like me,' the old man said, almost apologetically. 'I was cross … well … angry. Angry at everything. Angry with everybody. Your mum was the best … the best … but then I … '

'Then you what?' Ben said.

The old man looked out to sea.

'I've led a very lonely life … very lonely. And it was all my own fault. I regret it now, but …'

Ben waited quietly. He couldn't think what to say.

'And now it's too late.'

'How do you mean?'

'I didn't want you to grow up like I did. I'd hate to think that I could have helped you … but didn't.'

'My mum never mentioned you … not even once. I thought you were dead.'

'May as well have been.'

'So you don't live round here then?'

'No … not round here … not round here.'

The old man turned back to look out to sea. A dark cloud had temporarily covered the sun, and a slight breeze caused the air to chill. The breeze brought with it the smell of seaweed, and the taste of brine.

Ben watched the old man. He looked very frail. Shrunken almost. Ben guessed he had been bigger, taller, but age had withered him. The journey here … from wherever it was he had come, must have taken its toll.

Ben stood up. The old man turned back to see him.

'Can I get you a cup of coffee, Grandad?' Ben said, pointing back to the burger van.

'That would be nice Ben. Thanks.'

'Then you could come back … you know … come and see my mum.'

'I don't think so, Ben. It's kind of you to offer, but I don't think so. It's too late.'

Ben looked at his watch. He shrugged. It wasn't late. Mid-afternoon. He set off walking to the burger van to get a cup of tea. There was a bit of a queue.

Frank watched Ben go. He felt sorry for him. He imagined he could see the boy's life mapped out clearly. Maybe if Frank had come back earlier. Maybe if he had kept in touch with his daughter. Maybe if Sharon's partner hadn't left her. Maybe if....

Ben walked back holding a cup of tea in a Styrofoam cup. He'd guessed the old man would want milk. He'd brought a handful of sugar sachets and a wooden stirrer. He got back to the wall but the old man had gone. He looked back along the road, then along the coastal path by the beach huts. He couldn't have gone far. Ben would easily be able to catch him up.

Two hundred yards away Frank was working his way back to the bus stop. He was going as fast as he could. His knees were sending shooting pains up his thighs. The joints were crackling. The pain in his abdomen was spasming up through his back. He ignored the pain. He never took anything for the pain. It had become his friend. His pain made him aware that he was alive. He hoped that Ben wouldn't follow him. It was too late now. It was too late now.

A Day In The Life Of A Lido Volunteer
by Karen Hine

Hot and cold
Wet and dry
Llamas and stingrays
Rings and balls
Loo rolls and soap
Bin bags and recycling
Comings and goings
Stamps and passes
Tea and coffee
Milk and biscuits
Goggles and sinkers
Calls and messages
Credit cards and cash
Lifeguards and volunteers
Swimmers and sunseekers
Fun and games
Trips and falls
Wipes and plasters
Sun cream and coats
Towels and flipflops
Love and laughter
Chips and ice-cream
Sun and shade
Paddle and splash
Lido and Cafe
Happy and Happy

Christmas Eve, 1939
by R.E. Loten

Frankie sat in the corner of the Lido café, hands wrapped around a steaming mug of tea, her mood completely at odds with the festive atmosphere that pervaded the room. Brightly coloured decorations hung from the ceiling and the soothing strains of *Silent Night* came from the gramophone in the corner. Tears pricked at her eyes. *It's not fair. Just because Addie's a few years older, doesn't mean she's more capable than me.*

Thinking about her sister only brought more tears to her eyes. This time they were about more than the injustice of her situation. She missed Adelaide. It was nice having a bedroom to herself for once, but it felt odd waking up and not seeing her sister's face across the room. *They could at least have given me a chance to prove myself. They didn't have to send me home straight away.*

As soon as war had been declared, Addie had announced she was joining the newly re-formed Women's Land Army.

'We're going to need to grow as much food as we can,' she told them over dinner. 'And if the men are all going to be off fighting, they're going to need women to grow it.'

'But Addie, there are plenty of farms around here,' their mother argued. 'Couldn't you just go and work at one of them? I'm sure the Dawsons would welcome the extra help.'

Adelaide shook her head, her expression stubborn. 'I'll go wherever they send me. The Dawsons have plenty of help still.'

Lily opened her mouth to continue the argument but her husband's hand on her arm was enough for her to change her mind. Laurence Thompson rarely put his foot down, but when he did, his word was final. She glanced at him and he smiled gently before patting her arm. She stabbed the potato on her plate, focusing her frustration on the food instead.

Frankie looked at her father and saw he was now smiling sympathetically at his eldest daughter. *He knows. He must do. But how?* Frankie was sure her proud sister would not have breathed a word about what had happened, so was at a loss to explain how their father had found out that Addie had ended her relationship with Aubrey Dawson. She wondered if he also knew why and found herself fervently praying that their mother remained in ignorance. Frankie and Addie adored their mother and neither could bear the idea that anyone thought less of her than they did.

The party Frankie was sulking in the corner of had been Lily's idea. Her initial suggestion had been to have it at The Mermaid, but when the Lido café had been suggested as an alternative, she had decided that the evacuees would probably prefer the novelty of the pool. It would be far too cold to swim of course, but they would enjoy watching the crabs and eels swimming around in the water. They had planned to take in evacuees of their own at the hotel, but the Royal Navy had commandeered it instead to use as their onshore base. Lily had still wanted to do something to help 'those poor children' and the Christmas party was the result.

'I'd have hated it if you two had been little and I'd had to send you away,' she told Frankie. 'Those poor little mites must be missing their families dreadfully. I just want to do something to help cheer them up a bit. Christmas is a horrible time to be away from the people you love. Who knows when we'll be able to have proper parties again, so let's make the most of it while we're still able to.'

There had been no talk of a quick end to the war in the Thompson house. Lily and Laurence had lived through the First World War and Laurence's younger brother had lost his life on the first day of the Battle of the Somme – two years into a war that was meant to be over by Christmas.

'Cheer up Frankie, it might never happen.' Kenneth Ford slid into the empty chair next to her and he nudged his shoulder against hers.

'It already did,' she said glumly, aware she was being unfair. Her sister's friend was nice and he was only trying to help. It wasn't his fault the Land Army had found out she'd lied about her age.

'You can always apply again in a couple of years,' he said, tilting his head and pulling a face at her in an attempt to make her smile.

She grinned in spite of her foul mood. Ken always had the ability to make her feel better. She'd miss him when he left after Christmas. He'd joined the RAF and was off to Blackpool for his basic training in the New Year. Like her sister, he'd been a constant in her life and his departure was another blow.

'You will write to me when I'm away, won't you?' he said suddenly. 'I don't know where I'll end up but I'll want all the news from home still. Avonstow won't seem so far away if you'll send regular letters.'

'Of course I will,' Frankie said. 'I doubt there'll be anything interesting to tell though. I expect my life will be very boring once you've all gone off to do your bit.'

'You'll miss us then?'

'Every day! I'll sit by my window pining away until you come home again.' She laughed, suddenly feeling much better.

Getting up from her chair, she put her mug to one side and headed towards her mother. Aubrey Dawson might have described Lily as *no better than she ought to be* but as far as Frankie was concerned, there was no better woman in the world and if Lily wanted to give the evacuees a party to remember, then her daughter would do her best to make sure it happened.

From his seat in the corner, Ken watched her go. He would tell her, he decided. After Christmas. *I just hope she feels the same*, he thought.

(Background story from Book 2 of the forthcoming 'Avonstow' series)

Memories Of The Lido
by Jacqueline Buchanan

As a little girl in the 60's I attended St James infants and junior schools in Brightlingsea. At junior school one of the summer 'treats' was to go swimming at the pool. This, for me and many others I'm sure, was an event that to this day still haunts me!

The pool was wooden lined and was tidal filled/cleaned every two weeks through a sluice gate.

Once inside, the awful task of getting changed commenced. The girls changing was on the left and the boys at the top near the sea. The cubicles were tiny, draughty and many a time I ended with a splinter in my hand or foot… your clothes and towel then remained in a heap at the side of the pool… and so into the pool!

The steps into the water were wooden and slippery. The pool was lined with wood, which was dark, waterlogged and slimy. The water seemed turgid and was crawling with all manner of sea creatures. Eels and crabs being the most dominant, it was not unusual to feel something slither round your legs or nip your toes. Diving for the brick (life-saving badge) was a complete mystery dive, as you most certainly couldn't see it, so you'd be groping among the seaweed, crabs and slime. Inevitably, you surfaced desperately clutching an old shoe!

After 30-45 mins of (usually) cold, numbing, slithering and shivering we were allowed out: retrieve your pile, try and get dry, back into your clothes and shiver all the way home with wet salty skin and hair.

After the pool was renovated in the 70's, I worked there the summer I left school, collecting the money at the ticket window. My friend worked in the new changing rooms. You could present your entry ticket and get a numbered basket that was then hung on a rack for you to retrieve later (a vast improvement on the old system). The summer of '76 I was 17 and spent every minute the pool was open, sunbathing covered in baby oil for a quicker burn, laughing with my friends and flirting with the lifeguards.

Today's lido is an incredible testimony to the people of

Brightlingsea and shows what can be achieved with a united vision and determination. In 2019 I was a volunteer in the ticket office and plan on doing so again in the future.

To this day I have not swum in the pool since I was 11 years old! I dislike cold water with a passion and if I can't see the bottom, I am unlikely to venture in and yet I am super proud to have experienced and grown up with this legacy.

The Brightlingsea Tsunami
by Aria, Year 3

It was a nice sunny day in the summer holidays. I was with my friend, Sienna. We decided to go to the Lido. We had to wait a long time because it was the hottest day in half term, so the Lido was very busy. There were so many people that the queue was unbelievable. It was so long it went all the way to the park!

Finally, we got in. As soon as were did, we jumped straight into the pool. Sienna got our and reached into her bag. She pulled out a rubber ring. Then a toddler came over and 'pop'.

'I can't believe he did that!' Sienna screamed.

'Let's get some chips,' I replied, trying to cheer her up.

'OK.' Sienna sulked.

When we got our chips, we decided to eat them on the beach, so we left the Lido and headed for the beach. When we got there, we found a nice quiet spot on the beach and sat down to eat our chips.

We had a great view of the water, but then it started bubbling and swirling. The tide was going out but it was like something was sucking up the water.

'That's weird,' Sienna said.

'I know,' I replied.

'Look! That dog is hiding underneath that table!' I had to shout over the dog's barking.

We decided to leave the beach as too many suspicious things were happening. As we left, we noticed all the birds were flying away from the coast, far enough away for us not to be able to hear them.

Then, all of a sudden, it sounded as though there was a fighter jet and a train above us. Something bad was going to happen.

'I think we have to get out of here!' I said, worried.

'Yes.' Sienna also looked worried. 'We should definitely get out of here. Let's go to my flat.'

'That's a good idea, but how are we going to get there?'

'There are some bikes over there. Let's borrow them,' I suggested.

We went to her flat and knocked on the door. Her mum came out.

'What are you doing here?'

'Don't worry,' Sienna said.

We went inside. It took a long time to get up to her floor, but we finally got there and looked out of the window…

Below us, we saw unpredictable, salty shock waves. They were demolishing the whole town! We could hear them crashing and breaking beneath us and I could smell the salty, foam. The wind was crazy and it was lashing everything hard enough to flip things over. The beach huts were gone. There was shattered wood everywhere.

We were alone.

The Brightlingsea Harpy
by Beck Collett

I was eleven when I first saw her, though I'd heard her many times before that. I lay, floating on my back in a star shape, my pink and white striped one-piece (Dad wouldn't let me wear a bikini at the time, said it wasn't proper) contrasting beautifully from above with the blue tiles of the lido. The water lapped gently over my tummy, courtesy of Adam Brooks and his cousins trying to show off to me. I ignored them, as Mum told me to, and started to twirl in the water. It was a quiet day for the pool, though the sun was shining. A cold wind had arrived in Brightlingsea that morning, and many must have changed their plans. Not me, though, nor Adam Brooks. I closed my eyes as I spun, tuning out the boys' cries until all I could hear were the waves splashing in the creek – or maybe it was a boat on the lake; either way, the world was water and me. I was Amphitrite, Poseidon's wife, and queen of the water. I must have looked ridiculous, or magnificent, one of those, as I spun round and round with my eyes closed, and a goofy smile upon my face. Then, I heard her.

Her voice came quietly at first, steadily building, until she was louder than the water. I didn't want to open my eyes, for I'd read about her in a book from the library, and sort of knew what she looked like. I was a bit scared, being only eleven. It's a strange age to be, you don't really belong. That's why I read so much about the past, and the never was, and went to swim whenever I could; so that I had something solid to belong to, somewhere where I felt I fitted in. It sounds stupid, I'm sure, but I was always a little different. Maybe that's why she came calling to me that day. She kept on, and on, but I wouldn't look that day.

The following week, it rained on the Saturday.

'You're not going swimming today, Amy, surely?' Dad said, 'Can't you see the rain?'

'Duh! I'll get wet, anyway, Dad,' I laughed, and slunk off to get my things together.

It was near the end of the summer holidays. The lido was busier than I'd expected, a few families had come down, refusing to let the rain spoil their plans. I was happy to see it busy, but a bit worried they may scare her away. Her name was unknown to me. I read about three sisters, and she was one of them, but I don't know for certain which one. I always called her Ocypete in my head, and my lips mouthed the name whenever she called me, but I didn't say it out loud because she was my secret. I swam on my back for a while, eyes scanning the grey sky, when I caught sight of her. She was flying high, chased – no, followed – by a squabble of gulls, the weak sun silhouetting them as they squawked and cried at one another. I knew her straight away. I didn't shut my eyes this time, but kept watch, whispering her name over and over again, willing her to come closer so I could see her. The lifeguard's whistle rang out, shaking me out of my trance, and I looked away for half a second or so. Adam Brooks was back again and had been caught ducking one of the other boys. Idiots. I looked back to where Ocypete had been, but she – and the gulls – had gone. It was weeks before I saw her again. I didn't know it at the time, but it was to be the very last time I saw her alive.

We'd been away on holiday, so I hadn't been down to swim, or even walk along the beach, for what felt like an age. Finally, I was able to get free of everyone for an afternoon and raced off down Promenade Way on my bike. It was quiet, though the weather was nice and warm.

'Flying ant day,' Mum had remarked, 'be sure not to get bitten.'

Word must have gotten around, because hardly any families were there. Adam, of course, was there. He and his friends were crowding around one of the picnic tables, heads together and whispering. I ignored them, knowing they were planning something naughty. I dipped my head under the water, allowing it to creep into my ears, and drown out the world. Coming back up, I swam a few lengths, and settled into my favoured position of floating on my back.

'Hey, Ames,' Adam yelled, 'they got floats out today. Wanna go on the unicorn?' He pointed to a beautiful white unicorn, with multi-coloured braided hair, that sat gently bobbing by the pool side. 'I'll get her for you.' And he ran (the lifeguard blew his whistle at him for that, No Running!) and grabbed her, hurling the float at me as though she were a discus.

'Thanks,' I mumbled, and got on her as ladylike as I could. Some of the boys laughed, so clearly, I wasn't all that graceful. I felt a little self-conscious at first, but after a few minutes stopped caring. I hadn't been on a float since I was seven or eight and had forgotten how much fun it could be. That stopped with a sharp pain to my thigh, followed immediately by a wild hissing and bubbling in the water, and finally, snorts of laughter from the boys. I looked down at my thigh, expecting to see a bee stinging me, and saw instead an angry red spot appearing. The lifeguard's whistle blew, and I looked over to Adam. He, and his stupid friends, were trying – unsuccessfully – to hide catapults behind their backs. The cruel sods had shot me, and the poor unicorn, and were now being loudly told to go home.

'Sorry, Ames,' Adam yelled, looking anything but, and they tumbled out of the lido, their voices carrying off in the direction of the beach.

Though it stung like crazy where the pellet had hit, I wasn't bleeding, so didn't have to leave the water. The unicorn was pulled onto the side of the water, half deflated. I knew how it felt. I swam a few lengths front-crawl, but my heart wasn't in it, and I just wanted to go home. Just as I was about to get out, I heard a familiar cry. Looking up, her call grew louder, I could hear the anger in her voice, anger mixed with anguish. I didn't even stop to grab my things, or get dressed, just hauled myself out of the water and ran out onto the street and down towards the beach. I tried to keep her in my sight, oblivious to the people I guess were gawping at me as I passed by them. I could hear the excited voices of the boys growing louder, and I willed her to fly away to safety, though I knew in my heart she was too brave to do anything so cowardly. My feet touched sand, and I started screaming at the top of my lungs to the boys to stop, to leave her alone, but they were so wild they couldn't hear me. There they grouped, catapults raised to the sky, shooting pebbles up at Ocypete. Stop it, I begged, stop it, please, but they took no notice.

Reaching down for another pebble to launch, Adam caught sight of me. 'Ames,' he grinned, want me to get you a pet seagull?' and turned back without waiting for a reply.

'She isn't a gull, you idiot,' I cried, tears running down my face, 'you'll hurt her, Adam, please stop it.' To his credit, he did stop, but the others didn't. I heard a terrible scream, and a cry repeated over and over again. Ocypete flew away in the direction of the quarry, less steady, and slower than she had flown before.

'What did you mean that she isn't a gull, Ames?' Adam called, but I was already running back to the lido to grab my bike and go to Ocypete's aid.

Bare feet bleeding, and with a stitch in my right side, I peddled furiously along the roads, praying I could get to her in time. I approached the quarry and was surprised by the number of cars parked outside. Throwing my bike to the ground, I began to limp into the quarry.

'Can I help you, young lady?'

I looked up and saw a concerned looking man staring at me. 'My, someone I, she got hurt,' I stammered, struggling for air, 'I think she came here.'

The man nodded. 'What's your name?' he asked me in a friendly voice. 'My name's Ben.'

'Amy,' I said, rubbing the soles of my feet on some grass and wincing.

'And, your friend, Amy, what's her name?' I didn't know how to answer him without him thinking me crazy. He seemed to understand. 'What does she look like, then?'

I took a deep breath, and told him that she was quite small, and very beautiful, and loud. And that she had wings and talons. Even if I hadn't been stood there in a swimming costume, furiously rubbing my right side to try and get the stitch to go away, with my feet bleeding on the ground in front of him, I knew he would have thought me mad or playing a joke on him. I didn't dare look up.

There was silence, but only for a few seconds. 'I see,' Ben said. It didn't sound like he was cross or dying to burst out laughing. 'Do you know her name, Amy? Only she sounds like something from another world to me.'

'I call her Ocypete,' I said, 'she's—'

'A harpy,' Ben replied, 'is that right?'

My stupid, blotchy face gaped at him, and he laughed.

'Ocypete isn't the most common of names, she's one of three sisters, isn't she?' He nodded, as though answering himself. 'I'll keep my eyes open for her, I promise. We're actually doing a dig here, today, so we've all got our eyes open for wonders. Is there someone I can call for you, Amy?'

I shook my head, 'I've got to go back to the lido,' I gestured to my swimming costume, 'left in a rush, you see.' He nodded. I turned away from him and bent down to pick up my bike. 'Bye,' I said.

'Bye,' he called after me, as I tried not to cry.

When I got back, I explained my feet as having stood on something sharp on the beach, the red welt on my leg as a flying ant sting. Mum was satisfied with my excuses, and insisted on daubing it with calamine lotion, which made it itch like crazy.

We went back to school the following week. As I said, I never saw Ocypete again – only in pictures. I drew her obsessively, and each time she became more and more beautiful. For Christmas that year, Mum and Dad bought me a big book of Greek mythology – one of those books that are so huge and heavy that they come with their own ribbon bookmark. Sat, cross-legged on the floor, surrounded by wrapping paper, I opened the book where the ribbon lay, and there she was. Not a monster, not cruel looking, but quite small, very beautiful, and with wings and talons. I stroked the picture and felt tears pricking my eyes. Mum and Dad must have noticed, and went into the kitchen to make breakfast, Mum squeezing my shoulder as she passed by.

I'd never discussed that awful day with them, not in detail, but I'm sure word had got back to them. They were kind enough not to ask me about it, eleven being such a strange age to be. I turned twelve the end of the following March, just before the Easter holidays. We went away for a week, just a caravan holiday to Southcliff. We only lived a half-hour drive away, but Mum said it was a holiday, as it meant she wouldn't have to cook or clean for a week. She did end up doing both though, but at least we ate out a few times so she was happy.

We were close to Walton Pier, so Dad was happy, because he got to hang out and do fishing, and later on tell us loads of facts about the pier that we already knew.

He came back to our caravan one day, eyes shining.

'Ooh,' Mum exclaimed, 'did you catch us a big one for tea, love?' See? Desperate to cook!

Dad shook his head. 'Even better than that. Amy, that bird-thing of yours, you know the one?'

'Ocypete, you mean,' I said, with a withering look, 'she's a harpy. Actually, she was believed to—'

Dad cut me off. 'Yes, well, *her*. Well, I was talking to a man on the pier earlier, and he's big on archaeology. He said they did a big expedition—'

My turn to cut him off, 'Excavation, you mean.'

'Expedition, excavation, not important. Anyway, he's telling me about this dig they last year did down the quarry near us,' (Oh my God! I knew at once that was when it had all happened.) 'the usual stuff: tiles, broken bowls – Roman stuff, you know? But then he says, they found something else, something they kept secret.'

Me and Mum were so still, I don't think we were even breathing. Dad just grinned at me, with this annoying I-know-something-you-don't-know look on his face.

'What, Ted, what was it?' Mum asked, her hands fluttering with excitement.

'Ready, Amy?' he asked me, unnecessarily.

I nodded like mad at him.

'He said they found a little bronze figure of a woman – a woman with wings and talons. He said she was perfect, other than one of her wings looked damaged.' He looked at me expectantly, and his smile faded. 'You alright, love? Look like you're going to faint.'

The little caravan turned upside-down as I fell to the floor. I heard Mum scream, but she sounded far away. 'Ocypete,' I whispered, over and over again, 'Ocypete,' and I smiled, as the world around me faded to black.

Fun At The Pool
by Twinkle Childminding

While you are splashing
hear the waves crashing.

See the gulls gliding,
and people on bikes riding.

Getting that fresh Brightlingsea air,
better than sitting at home in the chair.

Stretching those arms scooping the water.
Come as a family, bring your son or daughter

Enjoy tasty treats in their very own cafe
Memory-making day after day.

Sweeter Than Chocolate
By Molly, Year 3

I can't wait for summer to come
So I can go in the Lido and have some fun

So come on, let's go away
To the Lido on holiday

There's swimming pools everywhere
But not like the Lido – the Lido's like a polar bear

But not so cold that it freezes your feet
So come along, it's a magnificent treat

It's like you're in the Queen's chair
Waiting for your camembert

So shout a cheer with a Lido beer
There's nothing more than the Lido here

There's lidos bigger than this one
But not as fun

I love the Lido because…
It's like you're in your favourite dream
I love the sea but…
The Lido is more than the sea can be

So come along, all around
The magnificent Lido, cold, wet and proud

It's like you're in a summer breeze

Think of chocolate in a pool, but sweeter than all!

The Star Of Peter
by Linda Taglialavore

As Peter reached to take the document from the police officer's outstretched hand, he noticed his own hand was shaking. Understandable maybe, but he worried it might be a sign of weakness, or even guilt. Surely the acquittal was his redemption. He should be bolstered, smug even, not trembly. He took the document, even though he knew what it contained.

'So, you will not be required to attend any court hearings or any further interviews.'

The PC's voice echoed down the tunnels in Peter's ears, round the corners, down the back of his eyes and into his brain.

'The case is closed and we, North Tendring Police, won't be pursuing any further enquiries. Liggens has been given a caution. Do you understand Mr. Bradbury?'

'Yes, I understand completely,' he mumbled, his tongue dry and heavy. 'And I cannot tell you what a relief it is to receive this news, officer. I've been living on my nerves for the past few months, it's been utter hell. There's not been a day go by when I haven't had to have a word with myself and say Peter, get a grip, you are innocent. Nothing is going to say otherwise. I believe in the justice system in this country. Not guilty until proven otherwise.'

Peter thought he saw a flicker of a smile cross the PC's face.

'Well sir, perhaps keep in mind that in future it would be better if you didn't befriend teenagers. Especially in the park in the evenings, as they are invariably up to mischief and it's easy for good folk like yourself to get involved in something that maybe you shouldn't.'

Peter felt small, and old.

'Yes, I see that now of course, but he seemed such a sad lad, down on his luck and everything. I only wanted to help. He sounded so convincing, you would have believed him yourself officer, I am sure of it'.

The officer was most certainly not sure of it. He was only sure that he would have told Matthew Liggens to get off home and stop bothering old people with sob stories about not having enough money to eat and then when the old man handed over cash, start shouting that he'd given him money for a blow job. Liggens really was a piece of work, and he knew Peter Bradbury would never live this down, the older generation finding this kind of thing particularly scandalous. Teenagers like Liggens on the other hand, wouldn't give a shit.

The PC shook Peter's outstretched hand, climbed back in the patrol car and drove to the station to complete his shift, whilst Peter returned to the TV and tried to concentrate on Emmerdale, but he couldn't settle. He wondered what Anne would have said. Probably something about victory and having a sherry. He should have felt elated and thought about having that drink in celebration but knew it would taste bitter. There was no victory, he was tarnished.

The next day when Peter woke, he decided he was going to try very hard to not think about the whole park thing. He was determined not to take those thoughts out and about with him, especially not today. He showered and made some porridge and as he placed the washing up in the sink, Anne was in his ear.

'That bowl needs washing up Peter, so you'd best do it before you leave, or it'll dry all crusty. If we had a dishwasher of course ....'

He shook his head at the memory. She'd had some crazy ideas sometimes. Since she'd gone, he'd tried to keep up with the housework but found it impossible to keep their home as she had done. He wrestled with the bed sheets on Mondays, found the vacuuming exhausting, and what the hell was happening inside the kettle. He stuffed his towel and trunks into his rucksack and left the house. As he stood to lock up, he heard Anne's echoey 'be careful' from behind the door. 'Don't worry my love, I won't be long,' he whispered to the door knocker that badly needed polishing.

He walked the mile or so down to the hard where the Harbour Master's dinghy bobbed patiently in the ebbing tide. The little craft had seen better days, it was true, but they could at least keep the ropes in good condition and the fenders could do with a clean. It's the little things that make all the difference. Peter stood, hands on hips and surveyed the sorry scene. He tutted softly to himself at the attempt someone had taken to tether the little rower to the jetty. Somebody clearly knows nothing about knots he sighed, that'll never hold. He bent low and retied the knot, properly this time. He walked on, his rubber soles squeaking softly on the weathered boards and bent to pick up some discarded crabbing line and a few bits of papery litter. He tutted again, and asked himself why? Why was there litter everywhere and who would pick it up after today? It made him sad to see his beloved jetty sullied by selfish visitors. Sometimes there was dog mess too, this made his blood boil, and he wished the Harbour committee would invest in CCTV.

'To catch them at it,' he'd exclaimed at the last AGM.

'It's a disgusting health hazard.'

His suggestion had fallen on deaf ears.

'CCTV is just not an option,' said old Jarvis.

What does he know? Peter's lips clamped together in a thin line and he called him a very very bad name, but only in his head. He wouldn't own up to saying it out loud. 'Peter please!' Anne would have said.

When he reached the Harbour Master's hut the door was open, and he could hear Elaine and Don chatting from inside. Up and down chit chat between man and woman; he missed that. The chat ceased and they greeted him warmly. (He wondered if they had been talking about the incident in the park?)

'I've just been looking at the little rower on the hard there.' He pointed towards the water. 'It's in a sorry state, not even tied securely.'

All three heads turned to look just as Peter's knot slipped and the little boat broke free.

'Oh, sod it,' Don yelled, springing out of the office with big strides.

'You see,' Peter said knowingly. 'Not even secured properly!'

He tutted and rolling his eyes dramatically for effect, left the hut.

He hurried away, passing the beach huts that stood together bravely facing the weather, and the tide, which was low now, exposed sandy cushions amongst the floor of pebbles. Through the Lido lattice he could see a few bodies flopping about, the sun from behind turning them yellow like massive goldfish. That wasn't a criticism, he reasoned, as he couldn't even swim that well himself, but they could at least make some effort. Move their arms occasionally or something. He could see old Jarvis, waist deep, chatting animatedly to another old coot. Were they talking about the park? After getting changed into his palm tree swimmers, (Anne's choice), he waded into the water, giving old Jarvis a cursory nod as he passed. One person he wouldn't miss. His breath caught as the cold hit his chest, but he carried on wading without flinching, for fear of appearing weak. He stretched out his bony arms, lifted his feet from the floor, and turning onto his back, let the water take him up to his favourite, and only swimming position, the star fish float.

Anne had been a good swimmer. He remembered on their honeymoon, how he had watched spellbound as she glided effortlessly through the waves. She made it look so easy, but Peter had always struggled. After repeated attempts at getting him to swim she had given up and showed him how to float on his back in the star fish position. This at least allowed him to go into the water whilst she dipped and dived around him, playfully tugging at his trunks under the waves.

'Hey you, pack it in,' he had laughed. They were both brown as berries on that holiday. Even though it was their honeymoon and they had spent quite a lot of time in their room, they still managed enough time at the beach to become like seasoned beachcombers. The sun seemed to shine every day; there may have been rain, but Peter couldn't recall any, and Anne had been so beautiful and so happy and such fun. Like she didn't have a care in the world, and he guessed at that time in her life she actually didn't.

The star of Peter, floated gently towards the deep end as he remembered when they were new and had walked together on coastal paths and sat a while to drink from a flask, and she would take his hand and kiss it. She continued to kiss his hand in this way for many years, but when the children came along, he noticed her kisses landed on their tiny hands instead of his.

The blueness of the sky, as beautiful as it was, exaggerated the floaters in Peter's vision. The ragged lines swimming across the clouds made him feel queasy. The opticians had talked about macular degeneration. He'd poo pooed that silly notion at the time, but maybe that would explain this morning's knot! Sadness suddenly overwhelmed him, and he felt warm tears slide down into the folds of his neck and he knew that today was the right day.

They had been happy, he supposed. She didn't want for anything, except that stupid dishwasher, and maybe he could have been kinder and bought her one. But it was too late now, and he wished more than anything he could turn back the clock and buy the damn thing. He would buy her a thousand bloody dishwashers if it would bring her back. He'd get a top of the range model too, not a cheap Chinese import. No, he would buy her a German one. 'They last forever Peter,' she had reasoned. His thoughts returned to the row, her voice had an edge to it, almost pleading, but he'd had a bill in the post that day to pay the subscription on his wine delivery. There was no money for a dishwasher when she could quite comfortably do it by hand and he had flatly refused. She'd turned back to preparing the carrots for his dinner and some tears plopped onto the pile of peelings, so he left the room. The guilt cut deep, making him gasp.

He let his neck muscles relax, the water line creeping ever higher over his cheeks, filling his ear canals with white noise. The palm trees puffed up with air as his bottom relaxed downwards and no longer in his star position his legs stuck upwards like a couple of twiglets. Peter began to sink, slowly and gracefully towards the bottom. As his lungs took an involuntary gasp and the water shot in, someone took his hand and kissed it.

Lido
by Mary Burridge

Definition: open air centre for swimming and sports.

Just like a beach – we have one of those too. But Beach Volleyball at Brightlingsea? More like Pebble Dash!

Our Lido really comes into its own when the tide goes out. All those hot summers with lots of kids to entertain and just muddy sand! What to do?

The Lido of course.

An essential commodity in landlocked countries like Hungary, which has more Lidos than anywhere else on the planet. I grew up with one, Ruislip Lido.
My dad was resident Lifesaver during the school holidays. We were always amazed how many people had heard of Ruislip just because of the Lido. But got rather annoyed because they always pronounced it 'Rooslip Leedo'! A large reservoir though, not like ours in Brightlingsea.

A specially built legacy to keep and treasure.

The Lido
by Selayna, age 9

A long time ago I went to the Lido,
where the swimming was so much fun.
I sploshed and I splashed and I jumped and I swam
whilst I played in the bright, hot sun.

I looked at the big pool that was right next to me
I wanted to go in so I did.
I was scared at first but was happy at the end
then I saw another swimming kid.

The swimming had stopped
so I went to get food.
I got a chocolate cupcake
which made the happy mood.

I went back to the stall
and I got some chips instead.
As I was walking back
all the memories filled my head.

I finished my food
and was very tired.
On the Astro I sunbathed
and it got really quiet.

I wanted to go home
because of the thoughts in my head.
As soon as I stepped inside
I flopped onto my bed.

Passing It On
by Lily Lawson

I was 7 the first time my grandmother took me to the Lido café. It's been one of her favourite places since childhood. Things had changed a lot since then but my grandmother was not one for resisting change.

She led me to the counter.

'What would you like. You can have anything, my treat.'

I chose caramel apple crumble cake. I wanted special and I had never had that before.

'That one.' I pointed to my choice.

'I'll have the same and two hot chocolates.'

The lady behind the counter smiled at us as she handed my grandmother a tray. I couldn't stay still. I was excited to drink from a mug and eat cake from a plate with a fork like I had seen the grown-ups do.

We sat looking out the window.

'We will have to teach you to swim Leah. You can learn here like I did. I'll teach you.'

***

My grandmother took me to the Lido every Saturday afternoon. Everyone knew her. They would stop and chat for a bit sometimes. I would wander and look at the photos, drinking in the history of the place.

She taught me to swim in the summer and we worked our way through the menu when it was cold. Hot cross buns, chips, bacon baps and, my grandmother's favourite, Victoria sponge.

It felt so special because I was with her. She wanted to share her favourite place with me, and it became mine too.

Until I left secondary school. Then I wouldn't swim outside anymore. We still went every Saturday; we sat in the café people watching. My grandmother made up stories about them. I wish I had written them down.

One Christmas she bought me a camera and we took photos of the building. My grandmother would do silly poses sometimes. I have the photos in an album.

***

My grandmother died ten years ago. We drove past the Lido on the way to her funeral.

Every now and then I come to the café on a Saturday afternoon, eat Victoria sponge and remember her. I like to write stories about the characters she created from the people who came here. I can hear her voice telling me what to say.

The Lido lives on and, in a way, so does my grandmother.

The Brightlingsea Tsunami
by
Sienna, Year 3

It was a really hot day in the summer holidays. I was with Molly and we went to Brightlingsea Lido. The queue was really long because it was so hot. It took ages, but eventually we made it inside.

Molly said, 'What a relief!'

We jumped in and it was so refreshing. Molly got her rubber ring and dived in. A toddler cannonballed in after her and bit Molly's ring, We heard air hiss out.

'Ooh,' Molly said.

'Let's go get an ice-cream,' I said, trying to cheer her up.

She agreed – I got chocolate and she got a strawberry.

At lunchtime, we left the Lido to have lunch. Molly noticed there were bubbles in the sea and white swirly lines on the top of the waves.

'That's weird,' Molly mumbled.

'Yes,' I replied.

All of a sudden, lots of dogs were barking, even the tiny ones who were hiding under the benches. The tide started going out, but not in a normal way. It was as fast as a bus driving at top speed. The squawking of the birds became shrieks. It sounded as though they were warning each other.

I whispered to Molly, 'Let's get out of here.'

'I agree,' she said.

We started walking home and I heard something that sounded like a train and bit like thunder. It got louder and louder. The waves got bigger and bigger and louder and louder.

'We need to go somewhere safe,' Molly said.

'Let's go to Victoria café on our bikes,' Molly said.

I agreed and we set off. When we got there, I was breathing heavily because we'd gone so fast.

We looked out of the window and the rain was lashing against it, unyielding. Shockingly, waves rushed up the High Street. It was catastrophic and I was petrified. I could hear an incredible booming noise. Foam and hung in the air and I could taste the salt. The wind howled terrifyingly, damaging glass and flipping over cars like they were toys.

We stared at each other in terror.

The Lido Café
by Donald and Elaine Woods

We ran the café, which is now the Lido café, in the seventies. It was very small at that time – there were no seats inside! We mainly sold drinks, snacks and ice-creams. It wasn't very profitable in those days and the field outside the café was a caravan site. We ran the café for two years and it was very different to how it is now!

Dragonsea
from a story by Arthur Loten

Once upon a time, there was a dragon called Zoddyac. He lived in Brightlingsea Lido. He liked living at the Lido because his friend, Charlotte worked there and so he got to see her every day. However, Zoddyac was an ice dragon and people complained that he made the water too cold for them to swim in. This meant that Zoddyac could only swim when no one else was in the pool. It made him sad that people didn't want to be his friend.

One day, another dragon called Yanani came to Brightlingsea. When he saw Zoddyac in the Lido he was angry.

'The Lido is a stupid place to live,' he shouted. 'The beach is much better because you can build sandcastles there.'

Zoddyac was hurt that the other dragon didn't like his lovely home and said the Lido was better.

'There's no shells to hurt my feet in the Lido,' Zoddyac explained.

Yanani was so angry that he breathed fire at the Lido café. The roof caught fire. This made Zoddyac sad because he liked to have cake in the café after his daily swim. Charlotte tried to put out the fire but it was too big.

'Help me!' she shouted.

People rushed to the Lido as the flames leapt into the air.

'Save our Lido!' they shouted.

Zoddyac flew into the air and used his ice breath to put out the fire.

'Thank you, Zoddyac,' Charlotte said. 'Now, what are we going to do about that naughty dragon?'

'Zoddyac could freeze him,' someone shouted from the back of the crowd.

Zoddyac frowned. 'That's not very kind, is it?'

'We could try to make friends with him,' Charlotte suggested.

Zoddyac smiled. 'I have an idea,' he said. He turned to the crowd. 'You complain that I make the water too cold. What about if we invite Yanani to stay at the Lido with me? That way, between us, we could get the water to the right temperature for you to swim in.'

'That's an excellent idea,' everyone said.

Zoddyac flew off to find Yanani. He found him on the beach looking sad.

'I'm sorry,' Yanani said as Zoddyac landed next to him. 'I didn't mean to set fire to the café. I was jealous because you had a lovely home. I accidentally destroyed mine when I lost my temper one day. It's difficult to make friends when you keep setting fire to things.'

'I freeze everything,' Zoddyac said. 'People don't like that either, but Charlotte is my friend no matter what. She'd be your friend too if you'd let her. So would I.'

'Really?' Yanani looked much happier.

'Of course. You could come and live at the Lido with me. We can swim in the sea together while the rest of Brightlingsea are in the Lido and then when they go home, we can play in the Lido together.'

'Would they let us?'

'We can make the pool hotter or colder for them. They'll love us!' Zoddyac laughed. 'So, what do you think? Would you like to come and live with me?'

Yanani hesitated.

'There'll be cake…'

Yanani grinned. 'How can I say no to cake? Let's go!'

The two dragons flew back to the Lido. Now they both had friends and a home they were welcome in.

I Believe I Shall Swim Today
by Mary-Jane Ng

I hesitate,
slightly conscious
of my near nakedness and exposed shape,
held within unfamiliar fabric,
concealed beneath a large stripey towel.
Cautiously descending the silver ladder,
first toes, ankles, calves,
then thighs submerged,
releasing my grip,
allowing myself to sink below the surface.
Self-baptism by full immersion.
Muffled ears pop as I resurface,
arms pull,
legs thwack and kick,
navigating my body through cold waters.
Weightless of thoughts and worries,
I float upon my back,
eyes blurred briefly with Monet vision,
cloud gazing
in our Lido by the sea.

'Of The Sea'
by Anne Beere

My name is Marina and Brightlingsea Lido saved my family from destitution.

I am as old as the beautiful open-air pool and when my mother Martha was expecting me, our family's future looked bleak.

My parents were poverty-stricken, my father was out of work and Britain was sliding into one of the worst depressions ever seen.

With twin boys aged two to feed and clothe, the prospect of another baby on the way must have been truly daunting.

When she sat in a rocking chair knitting at night, after the boys were in bed, my mother would put down her wool and needles every so often and sing softly to herself the reassuring words that she always used when times were tough:

'Something will turn up……I just feel it ……something will turn up.'

And it did. Mum would love to recount the day my Dad came bounding through the door, having been on one of his regular visits all over the town looking for work.

She told of how he came in, waving a piece of paper saying: 'You were right, Martha. You always are! Something has turned up. Look, here it is, some work, something has been sent to save us!'

He then scooped the twins up, spun them around and when he stopped, he placed his hand on my Mum's growing bump and made a vow:

'This little one will have the best, now that I will be earning, she will have the best food and will grow up strong and healthy.'

Mum had to take hold of his hand to steady him, he seemed giddy, not just from spinning the boys around, but from the excitement at the chance of being able to provide for his family.

'But Tom,' my mum had to ask, 'what is it? What is the work, what are you going to do?'

Dad was so overcome, he could barely speak. 'It's swimming, you know, in the open air, it will be lovely, the kiddies will be splashing around before you know it!'

'That doesn't tell us anything Tom, what do you mean, swimming?'

Finally, my Dad was able to explain, he had been given some work helping with the final stages of construction of a new lido in Brightlingsea, one of many to be built across Britain in the 1930s, as healthy outdoor pastimes became increasingly popular.

'Who'd have thought,' Dad used to say, 'the local council, you know, the bigwigs we thought were too high and mighty to help us, decided to build a pool and they needed men like me to put in extra muscle power to finish the work.'

Our manna from heaven had come thanks to the government's Unemployment Grants Committee which helped to finance desperately needed work for many local unemployed men.

I was born on June 4th,1932 and that same month saw a red-letter day, the official opening of the open-air swimming baths and nearby boating lake in Brightlingsea.

My parents gave me the name Marina, which means 'of the sea' to celebrate the connection between the water and my arrival. If there had been water births in those days, my Mum would have insisted on having that experience.

I later found out that only seven babies had been christened with the name Marina in the year of my birth.

It was an unusual name at the time and my Mum, who liked literature despite her humble upbringing, told me, if anyone teased me about my name to tell them it was in a play by Shakespeare and to ask them if they knew which one. I had the answer at the ready, it was the name of the daughter of the leading character in Pericles, Prince of Tyre. That would shut the bullies up, Mum said.

The lido was a place of pride for my parents, our family had thrived once that regular wage from its construction work was coming in.

When she was strolling by lido, with me in a pram and the two fair-haired boys bobbing either side, my Mum, usually a reserved woman, would call out, 'Thank you for saving us!'

This startled passers-by, but Mum would only smile and press on, head held high. Once an elderly lady, quite concerned stopped us and asked: 'What happened dear? Did some of you nearly drown? Are you thanking your rescuers?'

The lady was reassured with an explanation about my Dad and his work and how the money he earned had meant the difference between being destitute and being able to put food on the table.

We loved the lido and as we grew up swimming in the saltwater pool was the highlight of our summer days. Dad was never out of work again, unlike many men of his generation and our young lives remained untroubled.

Max At The Lido
by Jean Pickup

Visitors often think Max is the Lido cat. However, he just likes to visit us – he loves to sleep in the office or say hello to the people at the front of house. He also likes to pop into the café to say hello – he's not always welcome in the kitchen, but there's usually some bacon to keep him occupied! Max doesn't care, as long as there are people to say hello to – he's a proper people's cat. At the Lido he's confident of finding someone to stroke him and he loves being picked up. Seeing him draped around a lifeguard's shoulders gives our visitors the perfect photo opportunity!

Lido Attack
by Mia, Year 3

At the beach one sunny day, all was calm and until everyone arrived ready to play.

'Hello, I'm Frank the crab.'

'I love crabs,' I said to my dad.

The crab scuttled away. I followed it, wondering where it was going. It went straight into the Lido! I tried to follow it but I couldn't get in.

'It's locked!' I said to Dad. 'Why is the crab allowed in?' I looked through the gate. 'There are others in there too! We need to get in.'

'We need to tell people,' Dad said.

'I'll let people know,' I said excitedly.

My friend, Emeli arrived, ready to go for a swim.

'You can't go in,' I said. 'It's not open and there's lots of crabs in there.'

'OK,' she replied. She looked inside. 'There's an alligator in there as well. It's coming this way.'

'We need to get in,' I said.

'Look, two scooters,' Emeli said. 'We can use them to tell people.'

'That's stealing,' I said. 'I don't like stealing.'

'Do it your way,' Emeli said, 'But we need to tell people.'

'I found two people,' I said.

'Me too,' Emeli replied. 'This is Olivia and Molly.'

'Aria and Erin,' I introduced them.

'How are we going to get in?' Aria.

'I found the man who runs the Lido as well. He's coming with the key,' I said.

He turned up a few minutes later. 'I've got the key,' he said. 'Has there been a break-in?' He looked really angry.

'Yes,' I said. 'But not by humans.

He unlocked the gate and stared in amazement. Luckily, he had a dog lead with him and he very quickly leashed the alligator. We helped him put the crabs back in the sea.

Bunty's Adventure At The Lido Café
by Kim Lock

Bunty the Bearded Dragon lived in a tank inside the family home. He basked under the heat of the lamp, changing colour as he warms up. He was a very curious creature. When his young owner held him, he looked out of the window into the garden and wondered if he would ever go outside.

One day he heard the fading voices of his family and the slamming of the front door and realized that they had left the sliding door of his tank open. Bunty climbed out through the opening, and he smelled the aroma of food bubbling in the slow cooker.

He heard the familiar whirring of the tumble drier. He felt the unfamiliar cool breeze coming through the open fan light window. Bunty began to climb up the curtain holding on with his long claws, used in his native country of Australia to grip the trees. He toppled over the frame and landed feet first on the grass outside.

It felt fluffy and damp as he scurried across the lawn towards the cover of the evergreen bush.

'Phew, I'm safe here' Bunty said to himself. It was the first time he'd ever been outside.

The green colour of the grass looked vibrant, and the sky was a wishy-washy blue with white whisps streaked across it. The pale sunshine felt warm, but there was also a cool breeze. He dashed from his cover and under the gate towards the road. Would he stop at the kerb? Would Bunty hear the noise of any traffic? Luckily the road was clear as he scampered across safely.

He heard a strange noise and saw a large moving vehicle coming along. The large black tyres and shiny silver wheels looked amazing to Bunty. Then he jumped with fright as it stopped by the kerbside and the air brakes whooshed. Doors flung open to reveal the driver sitting in front of a steering wheel. 'Goodbye, see you next time' the lady said as she stepped out. Bunty made a dash for the opening before anyone could see him.

As the doors closed Bunty retreated under a seat and stayed very still and hoped no one would see him. If anyone saw a

Bearded Dragon taking a ride on a bus they would be startled. The bumpy journey left Bunty feeling a bit giddy, and he made a dash for it as the doors opened, even though the driver was pointing and saying, 'Stop that creature!' Bunty ran very fast before anyone could see him or catch hold of him. The air was filled with a salty taste, boat masts shimmered in the afternoon sunshine, glistening water lapped the shoreline.

Bunty blinked as he felt a sense of wonderment. 'Wow! This is a beautiful place'.

Then he heard voices with squeals of delight, a splash, coming from behind the wall. He followed the line of bushes and crunched his way over gravel through a small gap where he squeezed his scaley body under the wall and came out onto artificial grass where people seemed to be sleeping.

'Café Lido' read the sign over the veranda with small round tables and metal framed chairs. The smell of cooking wafted towards him making him feel hungry. If he moved towards the smell he would be spotted for sure, so he chose the other route around the perimeter with its blue-coloured wall, dodging the gaze of the people swimming in the Lido pool. He was just about to reach the veranda unnoticed, when he saw the Lido attendant staring straight at him with her mouth wide open in disbelief.

'Is that a Bearded Dragon?' she said under her breath.

Oh no, he thought, *I better get out of here*. He ran as fast as his little legs could take him. Commotion followed; people screamed and jumped up; peace was shattered. Bunty ran this way and that way, dodging the grip of several pairs of hands hoping to capture him.

Plop! Splash! He had run straight into the paddling pool. His instinct kicked in and he started to bloat his body with air to help him float on the surface of the water. The children splashed and screamed as they ran towards the edges. Bunty swam across the pool and clambered out exhausted and disorientated.

Instinct told him to run towards the wooden shed as the Attendant was hot on his heels. He squeezed underneath out of reach and breathed a sigh of relief.

That was a close call! Bunty thought as shadows fell across the gap and fingertips appeared, reaching to touch him. Bunty stayed very still, out of reach, and waited.

Eventually, the voices subsided, Bunty peeked out; the coast was clear. He then heard a squeak behind him.

'Hello' said a high-pitched voice 'I'm Monty Mouse'.

Bunty tilted his head from side to side to get a better look at this little furry creature before him.

'Follow me,' Monty said, as he scurried away into the darkness. Bunty followed obediently and was suddenly on the gravel again, crunching underfoot and sheltering under a bush; the mouse was cleaning his whiskers.

'Are you having fun?' said a different voice, coming from Gerty Grasshopper who was sitting on a leaf.

Bunty was startled and intrigued as this creature looked very similar to the food he ate. He moved towards it. Was this his lunch?

'We heard all the commotion and saw you scarpering for your life,' said Gerty Grasshopper and rubbed his hind legs together, making a clicking sound.

'I wouldn't eat him if I were you.'

Spinning around, Bunty saw a large rodent.

'Hello, I'm Rodney Rat,' he said, politely offering his paw to shake Bunty's clawed foot.

'Hello, I'm Bunty the Bearded Dragon and I'm afraid I'm lost and don't know my way back home!'

'Nice to meet you, I'm sure,' said Rodney Rat.

'Don't worry, we can help you,' said Beryl the blackbird who hopped under the bush to join them all.

'You seem to have had quite an adventure today by the Lido here in Brightlingsea,' she said and continued with her distinctive birdsong.

'I wanted to see what happened outside because I've only seen the blue sky and green grass through the window,' Bunty said.

'How exciting!' said Monty Mouse. 'I've never been inside a house. What's it like?'

'It has walls with pictures of my family on them. It has comfy chairs that they sit on. It has delicious smells of food cooking, which they eat. It has sweet and floral scents when the clothes are washed.' Bunty began to miss home. 'I wish I could be there now!'

'You will always remember today, Bunty,' said Gerty Grasshopper.

'You have made new friends today, Bunty,' said Rodney Rat.

'We have learned about inside your home, and you've learned what is outside,' said Beryl Blackbird.

'Yes, I'm ready to go home now,' said Bunty, feeling tired and weary from all the running he had done.

The earlier sunshine was now fading, and it felt cooler. Bunty noticed a family far off in the distance sitting on a blanket on the grass. They were packing up their picnic basket to go home.

'Maybe they live near me?' Bunty said. 'I'll climb into their basket when they are not looking and get a ride home. It was nice meeting you all and I hope to see you again on my next adventure.' Bunty waved goodbye to his new friends.

'Goodbye Bunty; good luck finding your way home,' said Monty, Gerty, Rodney and Beryl.

Bunty looked through the leaves and twigs across the grass at the two children running around as their Mum and Dad were clicking lids onto plastic sandwich boxes and tying up a rubbish bag. He suddenly recognised Mum's voice as she called out, 'It's time to go children!'

He had heard that voice so many times before, in the mornings before school. It was his family!!!! He was so pleased to see them.

'There's my family!' He told his friends excitedly, as he ran out from under the bush, dashing across the grass towards the picnic blanket.

As he got nearer to the family, he was careful, pausing to hide in the long grass, so as not to be spotted by the keen eyes of his young owners.

When they weren't looking, he hopped onto the blanket just as Dad scooped it off the ground and tucked it under his arm. Bunty hung on with his sharp claws. Dad picked up the basket by the handle; the lid was wedged half open with a drinks bottle. Bunty let go of the blanket, gravity took over, he fell headfirst into the cavity of the basket, cushioning his landing on the softness of leftover sandwiches.

Dad's walking motion felt sure and steady as Bunty lay hidden in the basket. He knew he was safe and, on his way back home to the security and warmth of his tank.

Bunty had enjoyed the excitement of the day; startling the people by the Lido Cafe, his unplanned dip and swim in the cool water of the Lido pool, running away from being captured by the Attendant, but most of all Bunty had made new friends with the creatures he never would have met if he hadn't ventured outside.

Bunty was feeling grateful for having a warm, loving home and grateful for all the experiences he had outside in the open fresh air, with all the sights and sounds of the natural world.

Bunty would never forget his day out, but he decided there and then that he wouldn't venture out again.

'I will always be grateful for my family, my home and for outdoor adventures,' he whispered to himself as he was carried unknowingly by Dad to the car.

He listened to the children's laughter, Dad and Mum chattering together and their singing as they all joined in with 'wheels on the bus go round and round…'

Bunty knew what it felt like now he'd been on a bus, and he smiled to himself.

He felt the car motion come to a stop, felt the motion of being carried through the front door of home and into the room where his tank was.

As the children took off their coats and shoes Dad said, 'Anyone for casserole?'

'Me, me, me,' Mum and the two children replied as they eagerly scrambled up onto the bar stools to eat.

Bunty popped his head out of the basket lid, cautiously looking to see if the coast was clear. He'd had enough adventure for one day. He climbed out and across the floor. He looked up to see his tank with its warm light waiting for him.

His sharp claws once again helped him to grip onto the surface of the tank legs as he used the last of the strength in his body to haul himself into his tank.

Bunty was back home. He turned his face towards the heat lamp and basked under its warmth, changing to a lighter colour.

He felt very content.

'Is that a smile on Bunty's face?' Mum questioned, as she looked inside the tank where Bunty was sitting with his eyes closed, memories of the day whirling around in his brain.

'It certainly looks like it,' Dad replied, noticing the sliding glass door of the tank was open.

'Looks like Bunty's door has been open all day. It's lucky he didn't escape. He obviously likes it in there with his heat lamp and being fed fresh food every day.'

Dad had a fresh grasshopper held in plastic tweezers ready to feed Bunty. He leaned through the opening and offered Bunty his food.

Bunty opened one eye and peered at the food he would usually be eager to take, but for some reason he just didn't feel very hungry.

Dad was puzzled, so he offered Bunty a tasty green leaf instead.

Bunty grabbed it with his claws and gobbled it up immediately.

'Everyone! Let's not forget to close Bunty's tank door please,' Dad said, sliding the door closed.

'Night, night Bunty.'

The timer on the light switched off and Bunty fell fast asleep.

Panic At The Pool
by Linda Moir

It was a pleasant summer's day, perfect for our day out. Several members of my extended family had 'bagged' their usual spot beside the swimming pool. (Lido was a much later title). Each had their own particular role for the day designated by Grandma, the matriarch of the family.

'Best that way,' said Grandma. 'Don't want to be in a muddle all day.'

Roles rarely changed and went something like this: Grandma in charge of food, Grandad in charge of bags and valuables. Mothers in charge of calamine lotion, sticky plasters, clothes and towels. Fathers in charge of flasks of tea, safety in the water, rubber rings and the occasional trip for ice cream. Children, in and out of the water like leaping salmon. Every now and then Grandma would count children's heads like a worried sheepdog. She disliked the water, didn't trust it one bit. This went back to the swimming lesson given by Grandad during which she insisted he was really trying to drown her.

As the sun rose to midday so did the temperature. Grandad suddenly exclaimed, 'Rose, I'm going in.'

To which Grandma replied, 'Sit down, for goodness' sake you didn't bring your trunks. That will teach you to put things where you can find them.'

'Here endeth the lesson for today' muttered Grandad under his breath.

'I've got an old pair of shorts you can borrow,' said Uncle Jack, all 6ft 2in, 19 stone of him. 'You'll have to hoist them up a bit.'

Grandad appeared from the changing cubicles in the voluminous shorts and ambled off tugging at the adjustable waist cord. He launched himself into the deep end near the diving board. The inevitable happened and the family watched in horror as the shorts floated away. Thankfully, the pool was sea water then and a lot murkier than the crystal-clear water of today. Instead of waiting until the shorts were retrieved, a moment of panic gripped Grandad. He put his head down and started to swim his way towards the shallow end in order to get out.

'No, no. Get back. Back, back,' shouted the family, the children rolling about amid shrieks of laughter.

'What is it with him and water?' moaned Grandma. Some of the adults jumped in, forming a circle round Grandad and pushing him back to the deep end. My Mother had the presence of mind to take a towel in with her. Not a bath towel, but it was enough to save his modesty. I joined them and there we remained in a weird tableau. Two of the men rescued the shorts and tried to get Grandad's legs into them while keeping him decently upright. It was a Herculean effort as everyone was treading water. Grandma shouting instructions from her deckchair didn't help.

'Bill, keep your legs still.'

'Keep one hand on that towel, Bill. Remember it's Sunday.' We all hoped that fellow pool users would think we were rehearsing for some synchronised swimming event. I did my best to look like the then famous Hollywood swimming sensation Esther Williams, even attempting to smile underwater like her. This only resulted in choking and spluttering and did not add any dignity to the proceedings. Grandad was finally and successfully bundled back to the safety of the changing cubicles. Onlookers cheered and clapped, some women wiping tears of laughter from their eyes.

Grandma did eventually forgive him, and Grandad didn't mind being the butt (excuse the pun) for everyone's jokes. It was then ice creams all round and plenty to laugh about as a family in the years to come.

Any future swimming activity that Grandad did was in proper trunks tied up with an old tie for added security!

Maddy Comes Through
by Ron Hardwick

'Your usual thirty lengths of the pool before breakfast?' The lifeguard, clad in a canary-yellow jacket and seated on his high stool above the water, chuckled to himself.

'I might try for thirty-one,' quipped Maddy, climbing down the steps into the pool.

In the Lido café, two men sat, sipping coffee.

'That's her,' said the shorter, burlier man.

'That's who?' replied the taller man, whose squint was even more pronounced when he peered out against the low sun.

'Her dad's rich as Croesus,' said the short one.

'He live in Brightlingsea, then?' asked the other.

'Who?'

'This Creesus. Foreign, is he? Don't like foreigners coming here, even rich ones.'

'Oh, give me strength.'

'What's the plan, then, Albert?'

'Shut up, Ted. Haven't worked it out yet. I need time to think.'

'You're good at that, Albert - thinking.'

'And you're a dunce,' said Albert.

Maddy completed her swim and climbed out of the pool. She towelled herself down all over her well-proportioned figure. The morning was already warming up nicely and she was looking forward to her pot of tea at the café.

'Maddy, I'm glad I caught you. You fit and able?'

'Hello, Mike. Fit and able for what?'

'The final of the ladies' pie-eating contest.'

'Oh, that. Of course.'

'It's at midnight tonight, don't forget, in the lido cafe. Make sure you starve yourself all day.'

'Don't worry, Mike. I'll be in good trim.'

It was fair to say that Maddy had a good appetite. It hardly showed, for she was an attractive, fully rounded woman of twenty-eight, and not in the least obese. She could wolf down her pies quickly, though, and Mike had high hopes of her winning the contest, although there was competition - Nessa MacPeake, for example, the human dustbin, who, if you stood on her foot, you might well expect the top of her head to flip open.

The lido, a charitable trust run by volunteers, often created interesting contests to engage the people of the town and to raise much-needed cash, and the pie-eating contest was one such ingenious idea. The local butcher agreed to donate the meat pies, in exchange for some publicity. Whoever consumed her meat pie the quickest was deemed to be the winner.

The idea of a midnight contest had been Mike's. He thought it added a slight frisson to the contest that would be missing if it took place during the daylight hours. He was an aficionado of the Billy Bunter stories, in which the Fat Owl of the Remove often indulged himself with purloined tuck at midnight in the box room of Greyfriars school.

'We'll have to follow her and find out her routine,' said Albert.

'What about our lunch?'

'Forget about lunch. We have to follow her like basset-hounds, lying low, keeping out of sight. We can't think of food.'

'We could take sandwiches,' said Ted.

'I give up,' said Albert.

Maddy's father was in the stockbroking line and had amassed a not inconsiderable fortune, trading in equities. The family lived in comparative luxury in a large, detached house on George Avenue. Ted and Albert, villains from Harwich, were keen to take advantage of the wealth of Maddy's father, hence their interest in his daughter.

'There she is,' said Albert, 'walking towards the lido.'

'What shall we do?' asked Ted.

'Stick close to her but don't let her see you.'

'O.K.'

It was eight in the evening and dusk was descending on the pretty Essex town.

Maddy often took a walk then. She found it cathartic. She loved the lido, and would spend some time every day there, even in winter, when it was closed to swimmers, although the café was often open during the day.

She entered by the side gate, which was unlocked. Many people brought their dogs down at night for walks, so to barricade the lido to citizens was against the ethos of the committee of volunteers.

The setting sun shone spun gold on the flat-calm water. Maddy walked around the largest of the pools, the one that has a wooded island in the centre. She wished she'd brought her costume, for she fancied a dip. The sign said the pool temperature was twenty degrees, just right for a prolonged swim on a lovely August evening.

'Grab her, Ted. Pin her arms.'

Ted did as he was bid, wrapping his arms around Maddy's substantial torso.

'Got her. Gawd, she's got more legs than a octopus,' said Ted, as Maddy kicked out at him. She wasn't subdued until Albert managed to put a large and rather dirty canvas bag over her head.

'Where shall we take her?' asked Ted.

'To the lock-up. We can tie her to a chair and then ring up the house.'

'I can't breathe,' said Maddy.

'You promise to keep your trap shut?' asked Albert.

Maddy nodded and Albert removed the bag.

'What the hell do you mean by abducting me?'

'Your daddy's rich. I guess he'll pay good money to see his daughter alive,' said Albert.

'Here, Albert…'

'Don't call me Albert, you buffoon. You don't want her to know my name. Call me Number One, as we agreed.'

'Here, Number One, I ain't getting mixed up in no killing.'

'Of course, there'll be no killing,' said Albert. 'Her daddy's bound to pay up.'

Together, they bundled Maddy into a lock-up near the yacht marina. There they tied the struggling girl to a wooden chair with strong twine, and went out to find a public telephone box, as neither of the villains owned a mobile phone. They telephoned from a box near Bumbles the Greengrocer's.

'You got the number, Ted?'

'Yes, I've got it writ down on this scrap of paper.'

'Hand it over. Hello, is this Maddy's father, the rich bloke?

'Yes. Who are you and what do you want?' replied a well-modulated, refined voice of at the other end of the line.

'Never mind who I am. Well, mister, if you want to see your daughter alive again, you'd better bring fifty-thousand nicker in used notes down to.... oh, hell, Number Two, where should we ask him to leave the cash?'

'The island in the middle of the pool at the lido?' suggested Ted.

'Good thinking, Number Two. Did you hear that, mister?'

'What on earth are you talking about? Is this some sort of game? If it is, I consider it to be in very poor taste.'

'It's no game, mister. Fifty thousand smackeroonies at midnight tonight, no earlier, no later. And don't inform the police. My friend here's got a gun and he's not afraid to use it.'

'I ain't got no gun, Albert, and I'd be dead afraid to use it if I had.'

'I told you to call me Number One! The gun doesn't matter. It's the threat that counts.'

'I cannot possibly lay my hand on fifty-thousand pounds by midnight tonight,' said Maddy's father.

'How much can you raise, then?' asked Albert.

'About three hundred.'

'We'll have to take an IOU for the rest,' said Ted.

'Right,' said Albert. 'Bring a bag with the money and your own personal cheque for the rest and place it on the island in the middle of the largest pool at the lido at midnight tonight.'

'How am I supposed to reach the island? The water's six feet deep. I can't swim.'

'That's up to you, mister,' said Albert. 'I suggest you hire a boat, ha-ha.'

'Wait a minute. I don't have access to a boat, but I do have a large inflatable swan. Maddy used to paddle about on it when she was six. It's in the loft. I'll need to blow it up. I hope the plastic hasn't perished.'

Maddy was a strong young woman. She started by fidgeting and worrying at her bonds, but that got her nowhere. She had an idea. She'd seen a film once in which the heroine was tied to a chair in a similar fashion and, by running backwards at great speed towards a wall, the heroine smashed the chair to smithereens and escaped. The first part of the exercise, running backwards, was easy, but the second immeasurably more difficult. It took four attempts before the timber gave way at the glued joints and she was able to shake herself free. She tried the door to the lock-up, but it was firmly locked and bolted.

In the lido café, Mike and the other organisers were laying the table with an oatmeal-coloured tablecloth and 'Welcome to Brightlingsea' crockery. There had been much debate about whether to serve the pies hot or cold, so the committee had compromised on 'warm.'

There were five competitors in all - Maddy, Nessa MacPeake, Dorothy the postmistress, Gloria the butcher's wife and one of the café assistants who, by all accounts, was lightweight and only there to make up the numbers. Mike was running a book on the result and had already gathered several hundred pounds for the Trust's coffers. He'd made Nessa evens favourite, Maddy two to one, Dorothy the postmistress five to one, Gloria the butcher's wife sevens and the café assistant a hundred to seven against.

Maddy's father blew frantically into the swan's nozzle, which was strategically placed under its tail. Fortunately, the swan hadn't perished from its confinement in the loft and it remained fully inflated.

Mrs Dutchburry, Maddy's next-door neighbour, on seeing Maddy's father striding out to his car with a swan under his arm, said to her husband, who was watching television.

'I thought swans were all the Queen's?'

'What?'

'Only Maddy's father's carrying one down his drive.'

'I wish you'd lay off the port at tea-time.'

'Come and look if you don't believe me.'

Mr Dutchburry hoisted himself reluctantly from his seat and joined his wife at the window. Maddy's father had by then placed the swan on the back seat of the Bentley and it was now hidden from view.

'I'd better call Dr Twemloe in the morning,' said Mr Dutchburry. 'Maybe you've got conjunctivitis or something worse.'

'We've time for a drink,' said Albert.

'Do you think we ought...?' replied Ted.

'Need to straighten out my nerves, don't I?' said Albert.

They entered the Yachtsman's Arms, a white stuccoed building standing in its own grounds.

'We're better sitting outside, under one of these gazebo things, where no-one can hear us,' said Albert. 'We got things to discuss.'

Albert ordered two beers and they sat at a table well away from the other pub-goers.

'Right,' said Albert. 'Here's what we're going to do. At twenty minutes to midnight, we'll open the door to the lock-up. You can tape Miss Maddy's mouth up with duck tape so she won't yell. We'll escort her to the island and tie her to a tree right in the middle of the wood. When her father arrives with the cash, you'll pick it up and I'll release her. We'll both wear these masks.'

Albert withdrew from his pocket a couple of black silk masks with holes cut for nose, eyes and mouth, and handed one to Ted.

'Just one thing,' said Ted.

'What?' replied Albert, peevishly.

'We can't swim neither. How are we going to reach the island carrying mistress Maddy when we can't swim?'

Albert's jaw fell like a portcullis, but he soon recovered himself.

'I know. We'll commandeer the swan.'

'How will Maddy's father cross to the island if we take the swan?' asked Ted.

'Never mind that. I'll think of something when we get there.'

Mike looked at his watch. It was twenty-five to twelve and there was no sign of Maddy. The other contestants were all there, stretching their neck and throat muscles in preparation for the task ahead. *I hope she's not going to be much longer. Maybe I should go out and have a look for her. I'll wait a few minutes and if she hasn't shown up by then, I'll go on a recce.*

Maddy's father swung the Bentley onto the road leading to the lido and looked at the clock set in the middle of the opulent burr-walnut dashboard. It read a quarter to twelve. He pulled up against the kerb and switched off the motor, glancing cautiously around him as he emerged from the car, swan under one arm, moneybag under the other.

Maddy heard the key turn in the lock and the door open. She rushed headlong at her kidnappers but tripped over a lifebelt lying on the floor and fell flat on her face, whence she was easily overpowered.

'That's it, Number Two! Lifebelts. There's another one over there. We wade over to the island and the lifebelts will keep us afloat.'

'What, in our togs?'

'No. We'll strip to our underpants. You idiot, of course we'll still be wearing our clothes. Does it matter?'

'But this is my best suit.'

'We'll have enough to buy you twenty suits. Come on. Don't forget to put your mask on.'

They picked up a lifebelt each and propelled the groggy Maddy towards the pool.

Mike was seriously worried. There were only ten minutes to go until the start of the contest and the pies were already warming in the oven. *I have to find her. I've bet twenty quid that she wins. He left the café and started off towards the largest of the three pools.*

Maddy's father removed his shoes and socks, rolled up his trouser-legs and paddled with his hands over to the island on the back of the inflatable swan. He put the moneybag down and waited.

Albert, Ted and Maddy arrived shortly after. The trio jumped into the water. The lifebelts kept the kidnappers buoyant, but the floor of the pool was slippery for those unfortunate enough to be wearing leather-soled shoes, which Albert and Ted were. Albert slipped first and dragged Ted down with him. Somehow, Albert lost his lifebelt and fell to the bottom.

'Number One's drowning. Help,' gurgled Ted.

Maddy broke loose, swam strongly around, dived down and pulled the now unconscious Albert to the side of the pool.

'Get him up, Mike,' she said. 'Artificial respiration.'

Mike dragged Albert onto the poolside and proceeded to pump the prostrate Albert's arms up and down like a Texan oil derrick.

Maddy's father picked up the ransom money and paddled the swan back over to the path.

Maddy dived fearlessly back in and rescued Ted, whose mask was now on back to front. It was easy for Maddy's father to give him a punch in the solar plexus that laid him out cold.

'Call the Police, Dad,' said Maddy. 'Got to go. Got a contest to win.'

It was a foregone conclusion. Because of everything that had happened to her, Maddy was ravenous, and she polished off her pie in twenty-six seconds, a British record for a woman. Nessa took forty-two seconds and the café assistant a good three-and-a-half minutes, though she did often dab at her mouth with a serviette.

As for Albert and Ted, they are both tending the Governor's herbaceous border at Her Majesty's Prison, Chelmsford, and will be for some considerable time to come.

Postcards From The Lido
by Elodie, Year 1

Dear Eric,

Our pool is very shiny and warm. My favourite thing to do is swim and do roly-polys under water. I get ice-cream and warm milk and marshmallows. My mummy sits on a deck chair and eats fish and chips.

Love,

Elodie
x

Mr Eric

The Igloo

Alaska

A Change In The Weather
by Poppy, Year 3

It was just an ordinary day at the Lido, a sunny day – a perfect day to come to the Lido. It was so crowded and the pool was so cold.

'I'm so dehydrated today. I need a swim myself,' David, the lifeguard said.

Suddenly, a thunderstorm slowly drifted overhead.

'I don't understand. It was so sunny a minute ago.'

A big, dark, charcoal-like cloud came. Lightning came rushing in. The wind got rougher and stronger and people started screaming.

'I want to try to save them,' Dave said, 'But I'd be putting myself at risk!'

It was pitch black, as if it was midnight. People were clearly worried about what was going to happen. Waves were coming in from the sea. Everyone was scared and panicking. They were lucky though – the water hadn't reached the town yet.

'I don't know what to do! I'm only supposed to be a lifeguard!' Dave groaned.

Thunder crashed. Everywhere the waves were getting too high.

'I must save people!' Dave thought. 'Everyone is in danger now. It's a total flood. The people of Brightlingsea are in real danger. They're all in trouble!'

Water spilled over the sides of the Lido pool.

'Oh no…'

Lido Volunteer
by Jean Pickup

We scrape, we paint,
We sweep, we clean.
We open.

Then greet and smile
And help and find,
A chair, a toy,
The answer to a question.

They swim, they splash,
They laugh, they play.
Happy people.
Happy volunteer.

The Red Polka Dot Bikini
by Jane Langan

It's good for you, she said. It staves off dementia, heart attacks and really gets the blood flowing.

'Fuck off.'

I am thigh high in freezing cold water. How did this happen?

I remember the night before, 'Yeah, it'll be great. Cozzies on and we'll just jump in. We could go once a week; we'll all be fit as fiddles in no time!'

Who said that? I know it wasn't me. Was it Shaz? Of course it was Shaz, always with the mad cap schemes. When we were several Proseccos in and we were all yay! Fun! Let's do it.

I glare at Shaz, who I can see swimming off towards the other end of the Lido. Her fat bottom covered in red polka dots. I hate her. I hate her goggles, her podgy arms, breast stroking away from me. I look to my right and see Karen. She looks blue. Her hands are crossed across her tiny chest. I can see her hip bones through her Speedo swimming costume that has clearly been brought for the occasion. It looks like her goosebumps have goosebumps, Jesus…are her teeth chattering. It's not that cold. I look at her and out of sheer bloody-mindedness decide I should just go for it. I don't want to look like Karen. No one wants that.

As my tits hit the water, I feel my nipples shoot out in freezing erectness. Fuckity fuck. Just keep swimming, Dory has a lot to answer for from those Nemo films… Just keep swimming… Shaz is waving at me from the deep end. I watch her bingo wings wobble, like the tiny waves made by the breeze on the water's surface. I slowly swim towards her.

'Isn't this just brilliant, I feel so alive!' Her nose is bright pink and she is beaming at me as her blonde curls sag down either side of her face.

'Yeah, brilliant.' I manage. I glare at her as I get closer.

I silently imagine holding her head under the water until she is found later in the day face down in the pool her blonde hair spreading around her red polka dot bikini as her belly dangles loosely like a cellulite-y whale beneath her. Hm, that cheers me up.

'Shall we do some laps together?' Shaz is still beaming.

'Sure, why not?'

'Maybe, we can get Karen to join us, she looks like an icicle up there on her own.'

'OK.'

We swim the laps, Karen eventually manages to get into the water, her solemn brown eyes look wet like they are going to cry rather than wet from the water, but she ploughs on, her teeth still chattering.

Afterwards, we go into the newly furnished café, it reminds me of The Great British Bake Off tent.

I am loathe to admit it but I can feel the blood pumping and feel better than I have for ages, I know I will sleep like a log tonight.

We order a pot of tea and two large slices of Victoria Sponge, because we 'deserve it'. I am just taking my first bite when Karen says,

'Where's Shaz, I thought she followed us out of the pool?'

'Oh, she had to go, something about leaving the dog for too long.'

'Oh. OK.'

'Hm.'

I smile and realise I have had a lovely time at the Lido.

Our Brightlingsea Jewel
by Lottie, Year 3

There was a dog called Fido
Who loved to go to the Lido
His owner loved their coffee and cake
She knew it had been freshly baked.

They loved watching people having fun in the pool,
Playing with water toys; it looked really cool
Splashing and sploshing up and down the pool
Young and old having fun together in this, our Brightlingsea jewel

Memories Of The Lido
by Steph Luckett

In the town of Brightlingsea the Lido is there,
for all to enjoy, to use and to share.

While you take a dip, see the gulls fly overhead,
perhaps you'll enjoy the Lido cafe instead.

2022 marks the Lido's 90th anniversary,
come and learn more about the pool's history.

Now filled with fresh water, once filled by the tide,
The splash area designed for fun with your child.

Memories to make in your local community,
down at the Lido in friendly Brightlingsea.

Unexpected Visitors
by Ziggy, Year 3

'Yes!' Lilly thought, as she and her parents reached the lovely Lido.

Before she went into the pool, she took a second to admire the sound of splashing, the cool breeze in her carob brown hair and the warmth of the bumblebee yellow sun.

All of a sudden, charcoal grey clouds loomed over the Lido. Thunder bolted down and pale white fins lurked in the water…

Without warning, great, white, menacing sharks sprung out of the pool, gawping at all the boys and girls in the Lido.

Lilly screamed. She had never seen anything like it.

She was in danger!

Swimming With Seth
by Zoe Martin

Ditched clothes show the way
To where the sparkling calls
Hopping foot to foot
The edge demands a pause

Until.....

The intrepid leap
Brings a gasp of delight
Swim, duck, jump, flail, splash
Then blue turns to white

Until......

Quick exit, towel wrapped
Warm snuggle trade
Hot chocolate clutched
Happy memory made

The Magic Picture
by Henrietta Edwards

Arthur sat in the café staring at the can of coke on the table in front of him. He was bored. He'd eaten his caramel apple crumble cake and his parents were *still* talking. *What is it about grown-ups*, he thought. *How can it take them so long to drink a cup of coffee and why are their conversations always so boring? I wish I was with my friends.*

A small white dog sniffed at his ankles and Arthur slid off his chair so he could stroke it.

'Hello Maggie,' he said, ruffling the little dog's fur. 'Have you come to see Tracy?'

Tracy was the café's manager and Maggie's owner. Arthur loved it when Tracy brought Maggie in with her. There were always dogs in the café, but Maggie was the cutest by far. The dog tugged at Arthur's sleeve.

'What is it, Mags?' Arthur laughed. 'I haven't got any sausages today, I had cake instead.'

Maggie continued tugging at Arthur's sleeve. When he stood up, the dog transferred her attention to the bottom of his jeans. Curious, Arthur allowed himself to be led to the far end of the room. Maggie stopped in front of one of the pictures that lined the walls. They were all by local artists and were for sale. The one Maggie had pulled him over to was a textile picture by Becky Jackson, his friend Wilf's mum. Arthur knew it well. He looked at it every week when he came for coffee and cake with his parents. It was his favourite of all the pictures.

Tilting his head to one side, he looked at the picture again. *That's odd,* he thought. *The waves aren't usually moving.* He stretched out a hand and poked the picture with his finger. Instead of the rough fabric he'd expected to touch, his finger went into the picture. He pulled it out in alarm. It was wet! *Well, that's interesting. I wonder…*

As he pondered the unusual turn of events, Tracy passed by with a bacon sandwich. Taking advantage of her being between him and his parents, Arthur gave a quick glance behind him to check no one else in the café had noticed anything odd, then put his hand back to the picture and pushed. There was a quick burst of light that made him clamp his eyes shut and when he opened them again, he was on the steps leading down to the beach.

'Arthur!' He turned and saw his friend, Elodie racing towards him. 'What are you doing here?' she asked. 'Where's your Mum?'

'I'm not sure,' he said. 'I was in the Lido café and I touched a picture and then I was here. Mummy and Daddy are still in there, I think. I don't think they noticed.'

'Come and play,' Elodie said. 'Mum's doing beach school so me and Josie got to come too. Emily's here as well, cause her Mum's helping out.'

Arthur let himself be pulled along the beach and soon, he was swept up in the crowd of children exploring the beach.

'It's good that you've come today,' Emily said, as she piled sand over Arthur's wellies. 'Lillia's mum is coming along with some art thing she's doing. Mum says she wants handprints and sand and stuff on it. Oscar, Isabelle and Tsvety have done theirs already.'

Just then Elodie's mum gathered all the children back together again.

'Right,' she said. 'Lucy's here, so in between looking at the seaweed, you need to go and do your handprints for her.'

By the time everyone had finished, there was a lot of paint on the sheet Lucy had put underneath the giant octopus they'd been putting handprints on. There was also a lot of paint and sand on Lucy.

'Oh no,' she groaned, looking at her hands. 'How on earth am I going to get this off?' She grimaced. 'At least it's almost done now. I've just got Rosa's left to get.'

Arthur tugged Elodie's sleeve. 'I should probably go. Mum and Dad might be worried.'

She nodded. 'OK. See you on Monday.'

Arthur ran back along the beach. How was he meant to get back into the café without being seen? His mum and dad were going to be so cross with him. He sat heavily on the same step he'd landed on when he arrived on the beach. He closed his eyes and sighed. Then he heard Maggie's high-pitched bark. He opened his eyes. He was back in the café. His parents were still at their table chatting. Tracy was just putting the bacon sandwich in front of the customer who'd ordered it. No time had passed since he'd left.

Good to know, he thought, as he went back to his parents' table. *I wonder where it will take me next time. Will it always be the beach, or did it take me there so I could be with my friends?* A thrill of excitement ran through him. Coffee and cake in the Lido café promised to be the start of many more adventures.

Postcards From The Lido
by Lillia, Year 1

Dear Eric,

I love the water temperature of the pool. It is warm. I like eating watermelon ice-creams. I like swimming in the pool with the floats. My mummy chills out on a lounge chair while I am swimming.

Love,

Lillia
x

Mr Eric

The Igloo

Alaska

Talk of the Pool
by Lewis, Year 3

Ruth came to school / to talk about the pool. / The pool / is cool. / The walls / round the pool are tall.

A Twist In The Tail
by Mick Galvin

The old man sat on a rock and gazed out at the water, his mind drifting with the waves that glittered and sparkled in the warm sun.

He liked it here, it was quiet, and no one bothered him, it was his 'Happy Place'. He tended not to stray too far.

However, once he had ventured up the nearby Creek to a place he now knew as Brightlingsea where there were lots of coloured huts and a tower, and even something called a Lido where people swam and played.

He loved watching the children splashing and laughing, although once, one of them went too far and was struggling. The old man had held the child up until others reached them, but he didn't stay; he was very shy.

He also loved to listen to people talking, not knowing he was there. He remembered the time he'd some Men arguing about Sea Monsters and Mermaids and saying they didn't exist.

Well, he had seen the Great Sea Serpent once when he was younger, *and*, he mused, *some not so great ones.*

But as for Mermaids, what did they know?

He closed his eyes, feeling the soft breezes on his face; relaxed, at one with his surroundings.

All of a sudden, there was a loud splash and a head popped up in front of him.

A girl with long hair and piercing eyes looked directly at him. *Now*, he thought, *this is a Mermaid.*

'Come on Grandfather,' she called. 'We're all waiting to eat, and you know we can't start without you!'

He smiled back at her, then in a flash he was gone.

A large green tail swayed for a moment in the sunlight, then slowly sank into the grey Sea.

Over To You

I said in my introduction that one of my goals during my tenure as Writer In Residence was to encourage people who wanted to write but didn't think they could. With that in mind, I'd like to close this anthology by giving you the opportunity to write your own Lido-inspired story. If you accept my challenge, please do send it to me!

Here are some basic story starters for you to consider along with possible genres to write in. Following that, are some more detailed story starters, courtesy of some rather talented Brightlingsea students.

- It was a crisp clear morning. The sunlight bounced off the surface of the Lido. Hayley smiled. Today was going to be a good day. As she hurried back inside the café, she failed to notice the storm clouds gathering in the sky behind her.

- 'Help!'
  David, the on-duty lifeguard was on his feet in an instant. Where had the shout come from? He frowned. Everything looked normal. People were swimming happily up and down the Lido. No one appeared to be in trouble. So where had the cry for help come from? Troubled, he sat down again, but continued to scan the water.

- 'Help!'
  David, the on-duty lifeguard was on his feet in an instant. Where had the shout come from? He frowned. Everything looked normal. Then he saw it. The hand waving frantically in the air at the deep end. He sprinted to the other end of the Lido.

- Hayley hummed to herself as she turned the coffee machine on. It grumbled into life and she left it to get itself ready while she put the jacket potatoes in the oven. Her pre-opening routine was interrupted however when a movement caught her eye. She looked out of the window. There was a creature sitting in the middle of the empty Lido pool. Opening the door, she crept along the decking for a closer look. *Is that…? It is… it's a…*

- 'Morning Hayley!'
  'Morning Fred. How are you this morning?'
  The old man looked sad. 'Not good. It's my…

- Chris entered the Lido café. *Oh good*, he thought. *Paula's working today.* He caught her eye and smiled shyly. When she returned his smile, he blushed. *One day. One day I'll have the courage to speak to her.*

More detailed beginnings…

It was going to be a good day today, Lily thought to herself. *We're going to the Lido to swim in the lovely pool to cool down. It's so hot today it's going to be busy.*

She arrived at the Lido and quickly hopped into the pool to cool off. Everyone was splashing at each other and swimming to the bottom of the pool and coming back up. Some people were at the deep end, diving into the sky-blue water.

But the fluffy clouds wheeled away and the sky turned to stone grey. The sea had much bigger waves and they got bigger and bigger. All the lifeguards got to their feet.

'What's happening?' said Lily.

She quickly jumped out of the pool. The water was getting higher and higher, then… BOOM! People were in great danger. It was a tsunami…

(Bella, Year 3)

Rosy was walking around Brightlingsea. It was a very hot day so she was going to the Lido. She got there and went into the pool. She could hear laughing. The pool was shimmering from the sun glinting on the Lido and looked like a big window. It was lovely.

At first…

Suddenly, the sun disappeared and darkness filled the sky. The water rose. There was a flood! It blanketed the whole of Brightlingsea…

(Norah, Year 3)

Prologue: Archie was running. He'd just stolen a diamond. He was being chased by the FBI. He had to get to the dock and down to his secret room, deploy the submarine and go. It was just a mile there now. He grabbed his gun and threw it in, then he backflipped in and closed the door behind him. He picked up the gun, deployed the submarine and set off in the depths of the blue sea. He changed into his civilian clothes and pushed the eject button. He flew out and the submarine folded up behind him. He put it in his pocket. Now he was going to be a policeman.

It was a sunny day at Brightlingsea Lido. Archie had the day off. There were lots of people and laughter. All of a sudden, dark clouds as black as ash came racing in like horses.
The waves got darker and violent going up to beach hut level now and it looked like there was going to be a flood. People started running to their homes and closed their doors and windows. People knew this was a bad one as the water level had reached the roads now.
Archie started evacuating people while the lifeguards were busy. When they took over, he took care of the sea creatures. But that was the least of their problems…

(Stanley, Year 3)

One day after school I went for a walk to the beach with my family and we went to the Lido. As we jumped in a Platapasaurus popped up.

'What's that?' Mum asked.

'It's a Platapasaurus,' I said.

'Is that a swimming dinosaur?' Dad asked.

'I think so,' Han replied.

'Let's go and see if it wants to play ball with us,' Jess said.

'I think we should,' Ry said.

We played 'fetch' with the dino.

'Aaaghh!' someone screamed.

A person was drowning. The dino saved him. To celebrate the rescue, we had a pool party. I rode on the dinosaur's back and it partied too. I laughed happily at her dance moves.

Suddenly, some Pteranodons flew above our heads. They swooped down and took us home.

(Emeli, Year 3)

My Lido Story

Printed in Great Britain
by Amazon

82428682R00058